the BUDGET KIT

The Common Cents Money Management Workbook

Third Edition

Judy Lawrence

DEARBORN™
TRADE

A **Kaplan Professional** Company

This publication is designed to provide accurate and authoritative information in regard to the subject matter covered. It is sold with the understanding that the publisher is not engaged in rendering legal, accounting, or other professional service. If legal advice or other expert assistance is required, the services of a competent professional person should be sought.

Vice President and Publisher: Cynthia A. Zigmund
Senior Managing Editor: Jack Kiburz
Interior Design: Lucy Jenkins
Cover Design: KTK Design Associates
Typesetting: the dotted i

Published by Dearborn Trade, a Kaplan Professional Company

Printed in the United States of America

02   03   10   9   8   7   6   5

Library of Congress Cataloging-in-Publication Data

Lawrence, Judy, 1948-
    The budget kit : the common cent$ money management
workbook / Judy Lawrence.—3rd ed.
        p.   cm.
    Includes bibliographical references and index.
    ISBN 0-7931-4128-1 (pbk.)
    1. Finance, Personal.   2. Home economics.   I. Title.
HG179.L338 2000
332.024—dc21   00-058944

DEDICATION

To my parents who inspired my skills and interest in managing money and ultimately my financial career through their everyday examples.

OTHER BOOKS BY THE AUTHOR

COMMON CENT$: The Complete Money Management Workbook (Forerunner to the current Budget Kit)

The Family Memory Book: Highlights of Our Times Together

The Money Tracker: A Quick and Easy Way to Keep Tabs on Your Spending

Daily Riches: A Journal of Gratitude and Awareness

Acknowledgments

My special thanks go to the following people who helped with the development of this new and revised version of *The Budget Kit: The Common Cent$ Money Management Workbook,* and always to those who gave their support and encouragement during the earlier times as this book metamorphosized through its *Common Cent$* years into the workbook you now hold:

- Cynthia Zigmund, Sandy Thomas, Jack Kiburz, and the other talented members of the Dearborn team who encouraged and supported this revision and saw it through to this great new format.

- All my many wonderful readers and clients who have used this workbook year after year and have shared their stories, ideas, and suggestions. Your shared insights continue to be valuable once again in this latest edition.

- Carol Park, my professional colleague and friend, who continues to inspire me with her work, ideas, and strong determination. Through her resourcefulness and generosity, I was able to make a smooth transition from New Mexico to California.

- My dear New Zealand friends Jessica, Misha, Inga, Ans, and Althea and my other beautiful Quest sisters. I am profoundly grateful for their healing wisdom and love and for helping me take the necessary leap that ultimately contributed to this new workbook.

- Mari and Chris Bauman, who inspired me to include the new Variable Income section in this workbook, for their hard work, determination, patience, and incredible success in managing very variable income.

- Shane and Jennifer Thompson who developed the great skill of prioritizing and planning variable lump sums of money. Their example was the motivation behind the new Windfall Planner worksheet.

Contents

PART THREE

Preface

We've all heard the saying, "If it's not broke, don't fix it." That idea has certainly applied to this workbook, which has been around since 1981 when I originally self-published it as *Common Cent$*. Over the years, there have been minor revisions and additions to reflect the needs of the times.

Now, as this workbook moves into its third decade, a new millennium, and a world of high-speed Internet answers to everything, I am pleased to say that the core concepts and worksheets provided in these pages still remain timely and effective. Even if you are starting to transition to financial software, you will find the overall budgeting process and the comprehensive categories to be very helpful and transferable as you begin the process.

Each revision, including this one, came as a result of many wonderful reader comments and suggestions, as well as my own seminar and one-on-one counseling experience with hundreds of clients over the years. I continue to welcome your recommendations for enhancing this workbook so it best fits your needs and helps you reach your goals.

My intention was and still is to provide a guideline or road map to get you started that is flexible enough to accommodate the many unique regional and personal situations that exist. The variety of worksheets throughout this workbook are designed to give you an overall view of your monthly and yearly finances at a glance. Modify them as needed to fit your particular needs.

One woman looking at this workbook at one of my seminars asked, "Where's the theory?" The "theory" can be found in almost every personal finance book on the market. I'll bet you have a few of those books on your bookshelves right now. Most of these books discuss volumes of valuable financial information. The authors usually encourage readers to establish a budget or spending plan and briefly discuss and show some examples. That still leaves the actual "doing it" part up to you, and that's usually where the procrastination, confusion, or fear sets in.

If you haven't been taught how to manage money and set up a budget, how would you know what to do? Just having money does not necessarily guarantee your ability to manage it. Not everyone has the time, knowledge, or organizational skills to set up a simple, functional system for managing all their daily, monthly, and yearly finances. That's why I designed and wrote this down-to-earth realistic workbook. Instead of theory, the *focus of this workbook is to complement the other financial books and give you a tool you can pick up, quickly read, and easily and confidently start to use at any time by just gathering your financial papers, pencil, calculator, and eraser.*

As a counselor, I originally designed this workbook for young families and for women who were suddenly widowed or divorced, had limited money management skills, and who often were intimidated by the whole idea of dealing with money. I have since realized, through my seminars and from the many letters and phone calls I have received from people of all professions and incomes, that managing finances is a universal concern.

What I also have seen become a major universal concern over the years is consumer debt. What an irony this seems to be after so many prosperous years of some of the lowest unemployment numbers, greatest economic growth, and highest investment returns this country has ever experienced. If there was ever a time you would think debt would be at an all-time low, it would be now. But it's not. Now, more than ever, the Debt Payoff Record section of this workbook is designed to motivate you. You can see at a glance your successful progress toward financial independence and financial control as you pay down, and ultimately off, your debt.

Once you take the time to start organizing and planning your financial affairs with these worksheets, the results will be extremely rewarding. Remember, this workbook is a tool for you to use. By itself, it will not change anything. With your input and your consistent and thorough participation in setting your goals, planning your expenses, recording and paying attention to your spending, and utilizing the many valuable sections, this workbook will help you create magic with your finances.

The magic will be in the form of financial peace of mind replacing financial chaos. Bill paying will be more manageable and automatic, which alone will save hundreds of dollars from late-fee expenses. Getting into the savings habit will be easier and more rewarding as you use the different savings records and watch your balances grow. Tax time will flow more smoothly when you use the tax-deduction records and have all the information you need at your finger-

tips. Keeping child support records will be more effective with the guiding worksheets. These records could provide that extra edge or make the deciding difference if you ever need to go back to court and verify any information.

And, finally, life will take on a whole new meaning when your stress level around money is greatly reduced and at last there is room for those other aspects of your life to come back into focus and balance.

Over the years, many of my readers have told me about the new sense of balance and control they were able to achieve by using this workbook. It has been extremely gratifying for me to learn how readers were able to purchase their first home, save their marriage, get out of debt, and start saving and investing money for the first time. Using this workbook has literally changed lives. I look forward to hearing how it changes yours. I wish you a successful and prosperous year.

Being recently divorced and new to managing money, I was surprised to find that doing these steps actually energizes me! When I write everything down and have a plan, I find I am no longer worrying about it. It really makes a difference!

Prologue

As I finished this edition and prepared to mail it to the publisher, a very special friend stopped me and said the book was not yet complete. She told me I needed to share my story of how I recently made a major mental, emotional, and geographical shift in my life and ultimately landed in my own paradise. After some consideration, I agreed.

My goal for my readers and clients always has been to uplift, encourage, and instill hope and confidence. I hope the following will inspire you to make whatever changes in your life you feel that you need to step into your own dreams.

GOING FROM THE DESERT TO THE VALLEY

Sometimes when things just don't seem to flow, and more and more of life seems like a struggle, I have learned it is time to stop and reflect. That time had come for me by the late nineties. Living in Albuquerque, New Mexico, was always a wonderful experience. The climate, uniqueness and beauty of the land, fulfilling friendships, and my professional budget counseling practice all were very satisfying to me. I never thought that I would someday want to leave or—more precisely—*have to* leave to really begin to thrive and move way beyond just surviving physically, emotionally, and financially.

I slowly began to realize that having loving friends, incredible respect in the professional community, and amazing hikes statewide, somehow were not filling me up. As one wise woman recently put it, I was continually on simmer in life, but never getting to the rolling boil. I had lived in the "desert"—and a beautiful desert—for more than 20 years and started to feel like I had taken the desert into my cells. Having grown up in the green lands and blue lakes of Wisconsin, I realized my whole being was starving for the lushness of green and water again—as well as the lushness of creativity, innovation, and passion.

Somehow much of my life had taken on the aspects of the desert. My clients came to me with issues of lack. As much as I loved working with them (and know I have impacted their lives in a tremendously positive way), it was becoming apparent that I was continually being around the concept of lack in my work life. As I hiked the foothills of the Sandia Mountains every morning, I took in the real physical lack that is represented by the desert landscape. When there is not a lot of moisture, plants learn to hang on to what little rain they get and adapt the best way they can. That means their branches, stems, and leaves all have a stiffness, starkness, and brittleness to them as they conserve what little moisture they have to stay alive.

I was seeing this same analogy in my professional world. My clients, with limited funds and limited options for bringing in more money (New Mexico has been ranked 48 in per capita income for many years), found the most effective strategy for their families was to hang on, cut back, and conserve whatever way they could. As practical as that approach is, and as often as we have been taught the technique of "spend less or earn more" from all directions, I believe there are times and places when the toll of that approach is too high. You soon start to believe that life is only like a desert and start to forget that many other landscapes exist. And even when you start to realize that other landscapes do exist, the thought of what it would take to get there can be way too overwhelming or scary. So you live life on a continual low simmer and never really get to that boil stage of abundance, opportunity, choices, and vitality.

Getting to that other stage would require change. Change, for the majority of us, is extremely challenging and frightening. And so, once again, staying with the familiar continues to have more appeal. That is, until the familiar becomes more uncomfortable than the fear of the unknown.

I had reached that point. For three years I knew, on some level, I needed to make major changes in my life. And I resisted. So many things I tried just never fully panned out. Gregg Levoy in his book *Callings: Finding and Following an Authentic Life,* talks about those callings, or messages. He tells stories of people taking up to five years before paying attention to what they needed to hear. That was helpful for me to know.

My turning point came when I woke up at 3 AM in a Chicago hotel in a panic attack. What was I going to do? The savings were going down even though I was a master at managing my money. The industry I was in was dramatically changing. There was no dependable, steady money coming in. The big chunks immediately got stashed for the lean times. I never felt I could really plan ahead. There was not a partner in my life to help support me emotionally, physically, or financially. I was not getting younger, even though I was blessed with good genes and excellent health.

*Y*ou do not get out of a problem by using the same consciousness that got you into it.
—Albert Einstein

How often I had heard the 12-Step definition of insanity—doing the same thing over and over and expecting different results. I knew I was living my life in the same place, basically the same way, with a few attempted changes, and wanting different results—a different life. I knew I had to change my life, but how? I was afraid to loosen the grip on any money I did have out of fear of not having any more coming in. At 3 AM there was no one to call as I sat in that dark hotel room in total despair.

Then the answer started to formulate. Guidance was coming through. I had a check coming to me that week and I knew I had to use that money to propel me in my new direction as soon as possible. The money would not be used for one more month of mortgage and the usual bills as that would only keep the same

old pattern in place. I had been thinking about moving to the Silicon Valley in California after a friend had planted the seed in my mind two years earlier telling me stories about the start-ups and stock options. Words I didn't even understand. I knew then I had to go there and immerse myself in the middle of that energy of abundance.

The planning began for taking a quick trip. I had a friend there I knew would help me out, but what about the expense of the rental car, flight, and meals? The next day I called that friend, Carol, who graciously extended her home to me for three weeks. By the end of that day she called me to say her friends wanted me to house-sit their beautiful home while they were on vacation and to feel free to use their car. The magical flow had begun. I always knew to trust when everything starts to fall into place easily. Next I called the Career Action Center and offered to volunteer for three weeks. I knew I needed to live as if I was living there and having a place to go every day. I now had a plan.

Two weeks later I was in Cupertino, California. It didn't take me long to realize I had just gone from Sleepy Hollow to the Epicenter of the Galaxy. The energy is off the charts. The traffic jammed. The housing and rental prices were too outrageous to even begin to think about. And still, I knew I had found my home. This was where I belonged.

Whatever it took, I knew I had to make the move. I had to totally change my life. It didn't matter that my computer skills were very limited. It didn't matter that my knowledge of technology was even more limited. Like a moth zooming to the light, I was choosing to head to the mother lode of computers and technology. If someone had told me I would move to Silicon Valley someday, I know I would have thought they were crazy. No way. Why move to the heart of the rat race? Yet there I was. I returned to Albuquerque and immediately put my condo up for sale in a market that was losing money. Next, I started going through stuff. It was time to clear out and move out!

I realized I couldn't get a *new* life if I kept holding on to all my *old* stuff. When planes are overweight with cargo they can't take off from the runway and fly to the next destination. They need to clear out some baggage. And so I cleared 20 years of files and piles, drawers, closets, bookshelves, rooms, and my office. I let go of old patterns of hanging on to everything, whether for future use or recycling, attitudes that no longer served me, meetings and organizations that were no longer a fit for me. I got rid of furniture, appliances, my bed, and even my car. Time to buy a different car. The furniture and appliances could all be replaced. I had let go of my attachment to things. By the time I did move out in the fall of 1999, I left behind one very small but full storage shed, a few things at friends' homes, and took with me whatever could fit in my car.

That was not all that I took with me. Most important, I knew I was taking the essence of who I was. And that was the most valuable asset of all.

So what did I finally do about that outrageous housing market? I knew if I went down that path, I would be so terrified of the prices I would never leave my bed. Instead I decided to be financially creative. I put the word out everywhere before and after I moved that I would house-sit. Over four months I managed to house-sit in a variety of places in between staying with my friend Carol. By the last house-sitting arrangement, not only was I living rent free in a beautiful home with a pool once again, but I was getting paid well to feed Toots, the cat.

What the mind can believe and conceive it can achieve.

—William James

So what was the key for me? During that whole process of knowing I needed to change right through to the point when I was determined to leave, I walked every morning along the foothills watching in my mind the video of the life I wanted to have. In my visionary world, the environment was sunny, lush, green, and fragrant. My workday consisted of doing satisfying work, making great money, and being part of a team of delightful, supportive, fun, bright, creative coworkers. People in general had an attitude of cooperation, appreciation, acceptance, diversity, creativity, potential, possibility, and vitality. The vision also included weekends of feeling the spray of the warm water as I slalom skied and enjoying the taste of the exquisite flavor of the salmon or trout on the houseboat trip. My energy level was high and sustained. I was happy, laughing a lot, thoroughly enjoying every experience and in total daily gratitude. In my core, I knew I was in total alignment and balance in my life.

To support this vision, I paid attention to all the signs around me whether from conversations, movies, books, birds, sounds, or even license plates. My journal is full of entries of one unbelievable synchronistic event after another. My condo sold to a perfect buyer. Money kept coming from unexpected

sources. Offers of placement for storing or buying my things conveniently came to me. Everything flowed once I had made a clear decision to move.

I have now lived in the Silicon Valley for a little more than six months. I absolutely love it and am living most of my vision. I am a total match to the people and the creativity that surrounds me. The learning curve is extremely steep. I now understand and appreciate the term "lifelong learning." Through it all I have been blessed with patient, supportive people all around me who continually guide me through the next new learning speed bump.

My nephew Dan once said, "Come to California and you will find what you are looking for." He was right. I did. Now, I remind myself to not put energy into regretting that I waited so long to take this risk or that I put so much energy into worry and fear for so many years. Over the years, I have learned to trust in divine timing. It's like the saying, "Taste no wine before its time."

I now encourage you to trust your own inner knowing. May my story or the following seven suggestions help you as you take your next step toward making a major change in life:

- *Find the balance between letting go and holding on.* Letting go can mean relaxing your grip on your money, material possessions, ideas, or attitudes. It may mean a new found sense of generosity or desire for service. Finding that balance means learning how to discern when it feels better to finally let go or when it feels more appropriate to hold on to your money, possessions, or behavior patterns and respectfully manage what you do have.

- *Create a vision of what you want.* Dr. Fred Waddell uses his "miracle question." If you were to wake up tomorrow and, by some miracle, your life was everything you ever wanted, what would it be like? How would it look, feel, sound, smell, and be? How would you live your life? Who would be in your life? What would you change? What would stay the same? Dream up your magical scenario and write it down.

- *Find a moment every day to spend time with your vision.* Nothing new here. I'm sure you have taken the classes and read the books on creating visions and making goals a reality. This time how will you actually *do* that? A daily walk, morning mediation, regular journaling? How will you incorporate the different senses as you step into this vision every day ?

- *Start letting go of the "stuff."* Clear the clutter in your life. Donate, give to others, have yard sales, toss. Do whatever it takes to start shifting the energy and begin the process of change.

- *Explore new experiences.* Take new classes, meet new people, try new hobbies, sports, crafts, books, CDs, Web sites. Change your routine. Expand your life.

- *Move.* Sometimes our lives can take on a whole new perspective by geographically being someplace new. Move to a new home or a different part of the town, your state, or even the country. Travel to different places. I read an article about the importance of a "latitude adjustment." Geography really does affect many people. I know that is why foreign travel always feels good for me.

- *Use the tools and techniques in this workbook to build your savings.* Using practical tools is one way to stay grounded and take personal responsibility for your life. Having savings provides security, freedom, and choices. As one friend put it, "When I have 'drop dead' money in savings, I have the freedom to leave any job any time without having to compromise my integrity." Following the guidelines in this workbook will help you create that freedom and ability to step forward into your vision.

May you too find the right time and the right guidance for creating and attaining whatever changes you desire in your life.

Many blessings,
Judy Lawrence

Introduction: How to Use *The Budget Kit*

*T*his workbook took some of the fear out of money for me. By setting up an amount I knew we could spend in an area, I didn't feel so bad when I was spending that money. I knew it was planned and okay. Before I was always in fear or guilt over everything I spent.

THE PURPOSE OF THIS WORKBOOK

The Budget Kit is designed to be easy to understand and practical to use. Because it is flexible, it can be used immediately regardless of the time of year or the condition of your finances. By following the guidelines in this workbook, you will learn to take charge of your overall finances by anticipating your monthly and yearly expenses, instead of always reacting to crisis after crisis.

There are two purposes for this workbook. The first is to help you get your financial information organized and keep proper records. With this workbook, you can keep records of your daily, monthly, and yearly expenses, medical costs, installment payments, credit card charges, mail order and online purchases, child support payments, savings, investments, retirement income, and much more.

The second purpose is to help you successfully plan and manage your finances. You can list and plan your goals; work out an estimating method for paying yourself (savings), your bills, and your monthly expenses; remind yourself of items you need or want to buy when extra money is available; and plan ahead for the periodic, but anticipated, expenses throughout the year.

HOW TO GET STARTED

Set aside a block of time so you can thoroughly review the variety of sections available in this workbook. These sections contain instructions along with worksheets that were designed to address many different needs. Each worksheet can be used independently or with another. Determine your own needs and see how this workbook will best fit them.

The many helpful worksheets in *The Budget Kit* are divided into three parts.

Part One helps you focus on where you are and where you want to be financially. Your *initial* time involved may be greater here as you gather and fill in the information. After completing this step, these pages become more of a place to revisit for reviewing and reflecting as the year goes on.

If this section feels a little overwhelming at this time, or you are very anxious to get started and want to jump right in and set up a spending plan, then move on to Part Two. Take a moment to skim through this section and come back later and complete it when it feels right for you.

Part Two is your action section where you plan, project, and record on a daily, monthly, and yearly basis. The bulk of your time and attention throughout the year will be spent in Part Two. You quickly will see how to anticipate those "unexpected" bills throughout the year, know how to plan out each month in advance, and learn where all your money is going.

Part Three is a collection of a variety of record-keeping worksheets for accommodating different individual needs. This is where you can keep records concerning child support income, mail orders, subscriptions, investments, retirement, savings, and other miscellaneous information. You also can record such expenses as medical and dental (including insurance reimbursements) as well as tax deductions.

Take some time to look through these three parts and each of these worksheets and see which ones will be more helpful for your particular financial situation.

PREPARE FOR THE KNOWN, THE UNKNOWN, AND YOUR DREAMS

By setting up your system for the year, you are planning ahead and getting a full financial picture. It won't be long before you see that you will need to have some system for saving money ahead of time for different purposes. Listed below are three different areas of savings I recommend you have.

1. Reserve account (the *known* expenses). After listing your major anticipated periodic or nonmonthly expenses throughout the year on your **Yearly Budget Worksheet** in Part Two (such as car insurance, home improvement plans, tuition, gifts, etc.), total these up. See the sample on page 26.

Divide this total number by 12 to get the monthly amount you need to set aside in a bank, credit union, or money market account for a reserve account. Remember, this is not your emergency money. This is a savings for money that will be due, only at different times of the year.

By setting this money aside each month, you will feel like you magically have extra money available when some of the bigger expenses (such as a family vacation or graduation) come due. These infrequent expenses no longer will disrupt your whole monthly budget or land on your credit card.

Enter this reserve savings category and amount on your **Monthly Budget Worksheet** in Part Two under "Fixed Amounts" at the top part of the page. (See page 35 for a sample.) Consider this part of paying yourself first as one of the fixed bills you pay each month.

2. Emergency account (the *unknown* expenses). There are going to be times when unknown disasters occur that create emergencies. Some examples are when the car breaks down, the home heating system needs to be replaced, your job position is eliminated, or your dental bridgework breaks.

The best way to have some peace of mind through any of these events is to know you have funds set aside. The guideline amount has been to have three to six months' worth of take-home pay available. Save this money in a bank, credit union, money market account, or mutual fund with check writing privileges.

Determine what amount you can realistically save each month (you may want to use payroll deductions) and slowly build this account up. Enter this amount under "Fixed Amounts" on the **Monthly Budget Worksheet** in Part Two. (Again, see the sample on page 35.)

Remember this money is *not* to be confused with the reserve account, which actually is being held for expenses that have already occurred or will occur.

3. Goals account (your *dream* account). An entire section in Part One is devoted to identifying goals and saving for them. This is the third amount that will be included under "Fixed Amounts" on the **Monthly Budget Worksheet** in Part Two. Initially, this may be a much smaller amount or even nonexistent until the other two accounts get started and have sufficient totals available.

By including your Reserve, Emergency, and Goals Accounts on the **Monthly Budget Worksheet,** you have a way of putting together and seeing your total spending plan. This process also reminds and encourages you to save and put funds aside regularly, offering you a system for staying in control of your finances.

GETTING A HANDLE ON SAVINGS

If saving is new for you or has been difficult in the past, remember the most important part of this process is *starting*. If you can only start with $10 to $20 per pay period or per month in the beginning, that's okay. Start with that amount. Use automatic payroll deductions to make this habit easier for you. The significance of this monthly step is that you are establishing a very critical habit as well as starting to accumulate some savings. Don't be discouraged with the small amount in the beginning. When you keep up the saving habit, the balance in your savings will gradually grow. As you develop a more effective budget, the specific amount you are able to save each month also will start to grow.

Remember to be realistic about the amount you can actually save in the beginning. Saving a small amount each month and leaving it in savings is much more productive financially and psychologically than depositing large amounts only to have to take money back out of savings each month to cover expenses. I have seen numerous clients with failed savings attempts and eroded confidence levels due to ambitious savings intentions but with no backup spending game plan. Every time these clients withdrew money from their savings for basic living expenses, they were subconsciously confirming their belief that they really can't save money. Once these clients developed a budget using many of the sections in this workbook, their savings plan stayed intact and grew in value. So did their confidence level.

One couple depends on the routine of planning meetings to keep their household of five flowing smoothly. "Every Sunday night when the kids are in bed, we sit down and talk about the finances. We make decisions about expenses and decide if we should spend money on something or save it."

WHO MANAGES THE FAMILY BUDGET

Who handles the finances in your household? Often one partner assumes and maintains the role of "Family Budget Director." Many couples fall into their respective roles because they are good at it, like it, or have more time, or by default when one spouse refuses. These roles often can be logical and efficient provided that the "Budget Director" is good at managing money. Once this pattern is set, it can last for years, unless some event causes the routine to change.

I highly recommend that each spouse be involved with the household finances in some way, even if that means trading off partial or full-time responsibility every six months, every year, or every other year. By getting involved with your household finances on some regular basis, you develop an awareness of your financial obligations, limitations, spending patterns, and overall current financial status. You also have a better appreciation of how expenses are going up—especially if you have a very active, athletic (and hungry) teenager. For example, the rising price of groceries and kids' shoes becomes very apparent.

This awareness is especially important for personal relationships. There may be times when occasionally the partner managing the finances must announce: "No, we can't afford that item or luxury right now." That news can easily conjure up a whole gamut of reactions for the uninvolved partner. Feelings of confusion and misunderstanding can translate into: "What do you mean? We were just paid three days ago. What are you doing with all the money?!"

If that person who blew up had first-hand experience with the bills and budget for the past six months, it would be easier to see the reason for the decision to cut back. It is difficult to know what you really can and cannot afford each month when you start losing that total sense of what it costs to run your household. You may not be as in touch with how school functions and last minute events seem to gobble up the discretionary cash, how computer interests or other hobbies tend to get more expensive, and how household repairs just manage to keep on piling up.

This mutual awareness by both partners is especially important if the designated Family Budget Director is suddenly in an accident or dealing with a long-term incapacitating illness in the hospital or dies or leaves due to a divorce. If the other partner is already familiar with the financial picture and the location of all the papers and records, then the trauma of the loss will not be compounded by the fear of taking on the new, often terrifying responsibility of handling all the finances.

Even without the traumatic circumstances, I have found many partners who confide that carrying this responsibility of having to make all the financial decisions alone for many years becomes a major burden. Many times both partners are very relieved when I suggest that the responsibility be shared.

I strongly encourage couples to work together or trade off the responsibility of paying the bills and keeping records. Decide what works best for your situation and then follow through on that decision.

FAMILY AFFAIR

Financial discussions are also important to share with the whole family. Remember, you are being the financial role model for your children. You can do this deliberately or by default. One way to look at this is to ask yourself: "If my children were now adults and handling their money pretty much the way I do now, would I be proud of how they were doing?" This question is more about a reality check and less about self-judgment.

Once you include the children in the decision process, you will be amazed at what insights they have to offer and how willing they are to cooperate.

If you are wondering how to get started, think of your family as a small business and consider having a weekly "family financial board meeting" on a regular fixed schedule. Set up the ground rules so everyone knows this is a safe and supportive place and time to express their thoughts and questions. It is a time for them to know they will be heard, not interrupted or put down. Establish an agenda where you will do your planning for the next week.

The following ideas are suggestions for how to productively use this family meeting time:

- Review your goals.
- Outline your spending choices and decisions.
- Determine charitable giving.
- Find creative ways to resolve money shortages or to utilize extra funds.
- Work out logistics of who will handle certain responsibilities.
- Be sure to acknowledge all the progress you have made as a "team" so far.

After a few months, or even weeks, you will begin to notice subtle changes everywhere—not just with the finances. Notice the shift in the family relationships, how the household is running, and your checkbook balance.

WHEN TO BUDGET ELECTRONICALLY

In this information age where it seems like everyone has a computer and answers can be delivered in seconds, you may feel compelled to use a financial software package to start your new budget. From my own experience with clients, I am not always convinced that electronic budgeting is the best way to *begin*—especially if you are new to budgeting. I encourage you to know yourself and your style first. Think about the following four questions:

1. *Do you work better when you see all the detail in one big picture?* If so, then scrolling around a screen and moving to different screens to pull the whole picture together may feel more confusing or overwhelming when you are just learning how to budget. Instead, looking at an entire year or whole month-at-a-glance page in this Budget Kit workbook may suit your style more comfortably.

2. *Are you impatient?* Many people just want to get started and don't have the patience to learn all the options available on the software programs. I see many Quicken users who haven't even begun to utilize anywhere near all the handy tools available to them. Consequently, they are not getting all of

the benefits or information that they could. In the meantime, they are entering figures and seeing reports, yet are not truly learning or understanding effective budgeting skills or concepts.

3. *Do you tend to procrastinate?* Turning on the computer, getting into the program, and entering the data may all become convenient deterrents for getting started or for keeping current. Some people find it easier to open this workbook, enter information, and be done. Again, think about how you operate.

4. *Are you computer savvy?* If you are, there is probably little that would convince you to write down information manually in the beginning when starting a budget. However, that is exactly what I am going to suggest *if you are just starting to learn the concept of budgeting.*

Even though you may feel you will get the same results by using your trusty computer, I have found that for many people there is critical tactile and visual learning that occurs with the manual approach that does not happen as effectively electronically. As you physically write down the numbers and visually note them and the surrounding information, there is a special awareness and understanding that occurs. After using this method for a few months and dealing with the planning and recording of the unique variations of some of those months, you will have gained valuable insight and understanding.

Couples have told me that something seemed to be lost when they shifted from manual recording to the computer approach too early. The planning, inputting, and visual awareness changed somehow. Instead, they had reams of reports and averages, yet did not feel they had answers.

Electronic budgeting does work very well, however, when started at the right time. Once the overall concept is experienced and understood and you see how the smaller monthly and day-to-day pictures fit into the bigger yearly picture, then almost any method will work.

Transitioning over to a software package at *this* point does make sense—especially when the computer does all the calculations for you. You also can take advantage of other conveniences, such as printing checks, banking online, paying bills online, and numerous other services.

One obvious reminder if you do convert exclusively to financial software or some program through the Internet is to keep backup paper records or always have current backup disks as a protection against any unexpected computer crash.

TAKE CHARGE OF YOUR LIFE AND MONEY

The methods and guidelines in this workbook will show you how to set your goals, watch your spending, and plan your expenses. You then will find that your bills are paid on time, more money is saved than you ever thought possible, your investments are off to a healthy start, your goals are being reached, and the stress in your life is reduced.

As you take charge of your money, you will notice this control carrying over to other aspects of your life. Your relationships with your family will become more relaxed and more time will be available to pay attention to other things in life besides money.

Best of luck as you begin your new money management program!

Part One

Net Worth Statement

Identified Goals Worksheet

Goals Savings Record

Needs/Wants List

One longtime reader wrote to say: "When I started keeping records it was like an awakening. In seven years I saved $100,000 thanks to your book. By the end of this year, which will be just over nine years, that number should be close to a quarter of a million." It's amazing how the numbers start to accelerate after a certain point.

This reader was exceptionally disciplined and motivated. Whenever he did not spend money (e.g., walk versus taxi, video versus movie, library versus bookstore), he would actually put that savings aside and record it in his book. On last conversation he still continues to feel no deprivation. He now *knows* he can buy anything he wants, and is very satisfied with how he chooses to spend his money.

As you fill in the following pages in Part One, you will see more clearly what you already have and what you still would like to have.

Writing down what you want in black and white is always a powerful way of becoming more focused and motivated in your daily living. Part Two will give you the tools for accomplishing your goals.

Net Worth Statement

An important step in gaining financial control is to take an accounting of what your total financial worth is. Every year, your net worth should be tabulated to enable you to review your progress and compare it with your financial goals. In addition, a Net Worth Statement is a valuable aid in planning your estate and establishing a record for loan and insurance purposes.

NET WORTH STATEMENT

DATE COMPLETED _____

ASSETS—WHAT YOU OWN

	Amount
Cash: On Hand	_____
Checking Account	_____
Savings Accounts	_____
Money Markets	_____
Other	_____
Real Estate/Property:	
Principal Residence	_____
Second Residence	_____
Land	_____
Income Property	_____
Other	_____
Investments: (Market Value)	
Cash Value Life Insurance	_____
Certificates of Deposit	_____
U.S. Treasury Bills	_____
Stocks	_____
Bonds	_____
Mutual Funds	_____
Limited Partnerships	_____
Annuities	_____
IRAs/Keoghs	_____
401(k) or 403(b) Plans	_____
Pension Plan/Retirement Plans	_____
Other	_____
Loans Receivable	_____
Personal Property: (Present Value)	
Automobiles, Vehicles	_____
Recreational Vehicle/Boat	_____
Home Furnishings	_____
Appliances and Furniture	_____
Collectibles/Antiques	_____
Jewelry and Furs	_____
Other	_____
	_____
	_____
	_____

Total Assets

LIABILITIES—WHAT YOU OWE

	Amount
Current Debts:	_____
Household	_____
Medical	_____
Credit Cards	_____
Department Store Cards	_____
Back Taxes	_____
Legal	_____
Child Support	_____
Alimony	_____
Other	_____
Mortgages:	
Principal Residence	_____
Second Residence	_____
Land	_____
Income Property	_____
Other	_____
Loans:	
Home Equity	_____
Bank/Finance Company	_____
Bank/Finance Company	_____
Automobiles, Vehicles	_____
Recreational Vehicle/Boat	_____
Education	_____
Life Insurance	_____
Personal (from family or friends)	_____
Retirement Accounts	_____
Other	_____
	_____
	_____
	_____
	_____

Total Liabilities

Total Assets minus Total Liabilities = **Net Worth**

_____

Setting Financial Goals

Jan was never successful at saving even though she made a great income as a loan officer. Once she started tracking her spending and learned how to work out a budget, it made a "million percent" difference in her life. She created a savings account to buy a house, which she never could do before. She practiced the "pay yourself first" technique, considered her savings as a bill, and successfully saved $15,000 in one year and bought her house. Now she's even more motivated about saving and is planning to invest in additional real estate.

Setting financial goals is one of the most important steps for gaining financial control. When you have a goal, you have the motivation needed to follow a money-management plan.

The worksheets on the following pages will help you identify and record your financial goals and develop a plan for reaching them.

To begin, ask yourself what is important to you. What will make you happy and/or be a significant accomplishment? Define your goals in specific attainable terms (such as buying a red two-door BMW instead of just buying a new car) and write them down. You then have taken the first step toward reaching your goals.

IMMEDIATE/SHORT-RANGE GOALS

These goals are any that you have identified for the next month and/or year. Your goals depend on your interests and your lifestyle. Perhaps you want to save your Christmas money in advance this year, buy a laptop computer, or pay off a major debt.

Do not forget your emergency fund. If you do not have at least three months' take-home pay set aside as a protection against unforeseen problems or disasters, this should be your *number-one goal*. Once you have the security of knowing you are covered for possible emergencies, you can comfortably focus on your other goals.

When you reach the goals you have identified in this section, you will have more confidence and discipline for the more aggressive goals in the Middle- and Long-Range Goals section.

MIDDLE- AND LONG-RANGE GOALS

Middle-range goals are those you hope to reach two to five years from now. Maybe you are dreaming of a new home, thinking of starting a family, or planning a trip abroad.

Long-range goals include plans beyond five years, including college tuition and retirement. By thinking about longer-range periods, you will make wiser use of your money. With time on your side, small amounts of money saved regularly for 10 to 40 years will grow tremendously. And if you pay closer attention to where you invest your money, it will grow even more.

FAMILY AFFAIR

If you have a family, bring everyone together to discuss their interests and goals. Children need to take part in this activity not only to give their input, but to learn from the process for their own adult years.

There seldom is enough money to reach everyone's goals. When Dad wants a satellite dish, Mom wants a piano, and Junior wants the latest athletic shoes or snowboard, compromise is necessary. Each member of the family learns to give and take and decide what is agreeable as a compromise. Rather than drop a major goal altogether, try delaying the deadline date.

One family decided to cut back and save for a car. In two-and-a-half-years' time this family of four with two young children saved $18,000. They did not consider it depriving when they chose to cut back on clothing and eating out and did a lot more buying at garage sales and auctions. Each month they also invested $300 without exception in a mutual fund as a dollar cost average approach. The best part was feeling confident in their ability to actually pull it off.

FILLING IN YOUR IDENTIFIED GOALS WORKSHEET

Once you have defined your goals and have written them down under "Goals" on the Identified Goals Worksheet, fill in the remainder of the worksheet. Number the "Priority" of each goal listed. Which goal do you want first, second, etc.? Which can wait a few months or another year?

What is your "Date Needed"? Six months, one year, six years? Every goal should have a beginning and an ending date. Once you have committed yourself to a time frame in your mind and on paper, you have taken one more positive step toward reaching your goal.

"Cost Estimate" helps develop your estimating ability and forces you to do some research. By calling, reading, or shopping to determine the estimated cost of buying a computer or putting in a pool, for example, your goal becomes more than just a dream.

If you have money in savings, how much of that "Amount Already Saved" do you want to use toward your goal? Write it down. Commit yourself to an amount.

"How to Achieve" is crucial. What are you willing to do to make your goal a reality? Will it involve working overtime or finding a second job? Will it mean trade-offs—cutting back or eliminating expenses such as movies, meals out, or smoking—so you can reach your goal?

How much will you have to save each week, month, or year to reach your goals? If you have a difficult time setting aside money for your goals, arrange with your bank for direct deposit from your paycheck.

The **Goals Savings Record** is a great place for keeping track of your savings for your goals. Take your

"Cost Estimate" figure from the **Identified Goals Worksheet** and write it in the space next to "Total Cost." Divide that figure by 12 to see how much money you need to save every month. Each month, record your savings and balance. You will be excited to actually see yourself coming closer to your goal.

PAY ATTENTION TO YOUR MONEY

If you have a strong desire to reach your goal and you *really* want your money to work for you, you must pay attention to what you do with your money.

Earlier, I mentioned having time on your side and paying closer attention to your money. For long-range goals (college, early retirement) where large amounts are necessary, these two factors are critical.

Let's say that you decide to save $100 at the beginning of every month for ten years to reach your goal. You could stash that money under your favorite mattress and have $12,000 at the end of ten years. Obviously, that method is not the wisest or safest.

If you had chosen to take that monthly $100 to your bank and let it sit safely in a savings account and draw 3 to 5 percent compounded daily interest, after ten years you would have made nearly $2,000 to $3,500 "free" dollars for doing nothing more than driving to your local bank. In the meantime, you would have saved $15,536.81 for your goal.

On the other hand, if you were to take time to find an account that pays 10 percent compounded daily interest for that same $100 every month for ten years, your reward for your research time would be an extra $4,995.61 over the 5 percent interest, or an extra $8,532.42 over the mattress investment, giving you $20,532.42 for your goal!

Saving $100 a Month for Ten Years

	Under the Mattress	3–5% Interest	10% Interest
Total Saved	$12,000	$15,536.81	$20,532.42

These figures do exclude the inflation factor; however, the more years you have to invest and the higher interest rate or return amount you get, the more money you will make. Read financial books, newspapers, and magazines, surf the Web, or talk to your financial planner, broker, accountant, or local banker to examine your options. *When you learn how to effectively invest your hard-earned money, you can be confident that you will reach your goals.*

IDENTIFIED GOALS WORKSHEET

IMMEDIATE/SHORT-RANGE GOALS

Priority	Goal	Target Date	Cost Estimate	Amount Already Saved	How to Achieve (Amount per month, second job, etc.)

MIDDLE- AND LONG-RANGE GOALS

Priority	Goal	Target Date	Cost Estimate	Amount Already Saved	How to Achieve (Amount per month, second job, etc.)

GOALS SAVINGS RECORD

Goal: IRA												Total Cost:	2,000
	JAN.	FEB.	MAR.	APR.	MAY	JUNE	JULY	AUG.	SEPT.	OCT.	NOV.	DEC.	
Deposit	167	167	150	160	177	167	157	177	167	167	177	167	Monthly Deposit: 167
Balance	167	334	484	644	821	988	1,145	1,322	1,489	1,656	1,833	2,000	**Total:** 2,000

Goal:												Total Cost:	
	JAN.	FEB.	MAR.	APR.	MAY	JUNE	JULY	AUG.	SEPT.	OCT.	NOV.	DEC.	
Deposit													Monthly Deposit:
Balance													**Total:**

Goal:												Total Cost:	
	JAN.	FEB.	MAR.	APR.	MAY	JUNE	JULY	AUG.	SEPT.	OCT.	NOV.	DEC.	
Deposit													Monthly Deposit:
Balance													**Total:**

Goal:												Total Cost:	
	JAN.	FEB.	MAR.	APR.	MAY	JUNE	JULY	AUG.	SEPT.	OCT.	NOV.	DEC.	
Deposit													Monthly Deposit:
Balance													**Total:**

Goal:												Total Cost:	
	JAN.	FEB.	MAR.	APR.	MAY	JUNE	JULY	AUG.	SEPT.	OCT.	NOV.	DEC.	
Deposit													Monthly Deposit:
Balance													**Total:**

Goal:												Total Cost:	
	JAN.	FEB.	MAR.	APR.	MAY	JUNE	JULY	AUG.	SEPT.	OCT.	NOV.	DEC.	
Deposit													Monthly Deposit:
Balance													**Total:**

Goal:												Total Cost:	
	JAN.	FEB.	MAR.	APR.	MAY	JUNE	JULY	AUG.	SEPT.	OCT.	NOV.	DEC.	
Deposit													Monthly Deposit:
Balance													**Total:**

Goal:												Total Cost:	
	JAN.	FEB.	MAR.	APR.	MAY	JUNE	JULY	AUG.	SEPT.	OCT.	NOV.	DEC.	
Deposit													Monthly Deposit:
Balance													**Total:**

Goal:												Total Cost:	
	JAN.	FEB.	MAR.	APR.	MAY	JUNE	JULY	AUG.	SEPT.	OCT.	NOV.	DEC.	
Deposit													Monthly Deposit:
Balance													**Total:**

The formula for determining the monthly amount to save for each of your goals is:
Total cost of your goal ÷ Number of months left to date needed = Amount per month you need to save.

Needs/Wants List

TAKING FURTHER CONTROL OF FINANCES

This Needs/Wants List is like a "wish list" that helps you take financial control one step further. This section is designed to be a guideline for those times when you have extra money but want to be sure that you wisely use your money on priority items versus impulse items.

NEEDS AND WANTS VERSUS GOALS

Needs, wants, and goals as used in this workbook are all the things that you would like to have but must wait until you can afford them. With your improved budgeting skills and money awareness, you know you will have the capability to eventually acquire these items.

The difference between needs and wants and goals is primarily in the cost and the significance of the desired items. Goals are more significant plans involving time and the gradual accumulation of funds for major purchases, such as an entertainment center, car, or home. Elimination of a major debt is also a goal.

Needs and wants, on the other hand, are the smaller-ticket items. These are the purchases made when extra money (known as discretionary money) is left over after paying the bills and putting aside money for your savings and your goals.

HOW TO USE THIS LIST

Throughout the year, you probably see or think about many things you need or would like to have,

but don't have the extra cash at the time to buy them. Jot down all your ideas on this Needs/Wants List.

Items on your list can range from things seen on Web sites, in mail-order catalogs, TV advertisements, or stores to activities such as the opera, a concert, or a ski weekend. Having these ideas written down also will make it easier for you to remember to watch for sales and list gift ideas as they come up.

At the same time, make a check mark either under the "Need" (necessities for your everyday well-being, such as food, housing, or medicine) or "Want" (which are nice to have, such as a video camera, jewelry, or theater tickets, but which you can do without if you have to) column. This way, you can make sure you take care of needs first when extra money is available. Record the source and cost of your items. When you are ready to purchase the listed item, the necessary information will be handy.

By using this Needs/Wants List, you start establishing priorities and identifying what you really do want when you have extra money. When you have an extra $50 (which you determine after completing your Monthly Budget Worksheet in Part Two) and a sale suddenly catches your eye, you won't be so apt to impulsively buy something. It will be easier to remember when extra money is available that there was something else you really wanted or needed.

A FAMILY AFFAIR

The ability to prioritize is a valuable skill for all age levels. If your children ask for something when money is tight, write down their wishes on the list or have the children write them down. Your action assures your children that you are acknowledging their needs and wants rather than saying that they just can't have something. In this way, children also learn to establish priorities, make choices, and develop patience. When money does become available, either from your budget or from their gifts or other money sources, your children can choose which item on the list to buy based on cost and priority instead of reacting impulsively to the first temptation that catches their eye in the mall, on TV, or on the Internet.

NEEDS/WANTS LIST

PARENTS

Date	Item	Need	Want	Source (store, catalog, Internet, other)	Cost

CHILDREN

Date	Item	Need	Want	Source (store, catalog, Internet, other)	Cost

Part Two

Yearly Budget Worksheet (Nonmonthly Anticipated Expenses)

Suggestion List—Additional Nonmonthly Expenses

Gift Giving Worksheet

Christmas/Holiday Expense Worksheet

Monthly Budget Worksheet

Variable Income Worksheet

Windfall Planner

Multiple Sales Monthly Planner

Debt Payoff Record

Debt Repayment Worksheet

Credit Card Purchase Record

Monthly Expense Record

Summary-for-the-Year Record

As a student, I used to carry my Budget Kit workbook with me every day in my pack. For anyone not used to figures, this workbook is an easy way to start. When I wrote things down every day it made me think, "Do I really need this?" "Where could I save?" "Is there something I'd rather spend my money on?" Writing everything down and seeing the total picture clearly gave me those answers and a real incentive to change.

Now that you are ready to develop a spending plan (a budget), let me walk you through the process just as if I were sitting with you at your dining room table, as I do with my clients.

The three boldface sections on the left, **Yearly Budget Worksheet (Nonmonthly Anticipated Expenses)**, **Monthly Budget Worksheet**, and **Monthly Expense Record**, form the keystone for the whole budgeting process for all households. The other forms are supplemental worksheets for households with varying financial needs. Over the years as I have worked with clients and talked with readers using this workbook, I have found that using these three sections in this order has provided the most significant results.

For years, readers have had their favorite sections. Some used only one or two sections, where others used nearly all of them. The purpose of this revised workbook is still to give you the same flexibility to pick and choose the sections that will work best for you. However, I want you to have the opportunity to understand the sections early on so you don't overlook one that could be particularly valuable for you.

The **Yearly Budget Worksheet (Nonmonthly Anticipated Expenses)** is the "missing link" worksheet that I have found makes all the difference in the world for people, right from the beginning. By starting with this overall yearly picture of where your money goes above and beyond the regular monthly bills and expenses, you see immediately and graphically why you are usually short each month, why you have so little to show for all the good money you make, or why your debt never seems to go down each year.

The **Monthly Budget Worksheet** is the next critical tool. As you begin each new month, use this worksheet to streamline the whole bill paying and budget planning process. This form helps you to anticipate all the bills as well as the majority of incidental expenses (hair perm, son's field trip, photo developing, etc.) so you know and can project ahead of time (before the month even begins) how much money you will need for the entire month. You will immediately see if you are going to be short so you have time to start making some arrangements and changes. You also will know what you can and cannot afford in terms of impulsive splurge events.

The **Monthly Expense Record** is the final and most important tool that lets you know where all your money has *really gone* for the whole month. This is your reality check on what your spending habits (like the coffee and bagel, CDs and books, etc.) are actually costing you.

I would be lost without my workbook. It's my bible. By keeping it next to the coffee and kids' money for school, the workbook is always handy. I color-code expenses for my kids and under pets I highlight the expenses of the horses in yellow and dogs in red so I know the real cost of each.

Yearly Budget Worksheet
(Nonmonthly Anticipated Expenses)

WHY A YEARLY BUDGET WORKSHEET?

This worksheet is designed to give you a general yearly overview of your irregular, occasional, nonmonthly, and periodic expenses at a glance. This method often provides a more manageable approach than the use of files, notes on the calendar, or even some software programs.

Having this information can prevent those pay periods when you finally have all the bills paid and give a sigh of relief only to be deluged the next day with auto insurance and property tax bills you had overlooked or not anticipated, which put your whole budget in a tailspin once again.

By having all this information as early in the year as possible, you can use it to make necessary arrangements ahead of time. How much money should you put aside in your reserve savings account for the dental work, could you postpone that new sofa, how can the vacation be less costly, is it time to cut back on the gifts? By thinking these options through ahead of time and taking action, you won't be falling back on the credit cards or loans to get you through the year.

FILLING IN YOUR YEARLY BUDGET WORKSHEET

Be patient as you go through this first form. It will require more time initially. However, the insights and information you gain will be well worth your time. Once this worksheet is completed, it becomes a valuable reference page for the remainder of the year.

To get started, grab your pencil, eraser, and calculator. Then gather up your checkbook registers, insurance papers, credit card statements, and any other related household papers that may give the exact or estimated amounts of expenses plus the months these expenses are due or paid.

Start at the top left, look at the expense category and, if it applies to you, move across the page to the right and fill in the exact or estimated amount under the month or months the expense is due. I suggest pencil because as you work this through, changes and new additions will come up.

See the Suggestion List at the end of these instructions to find additional and often overlooked expenses that may apply to your household but are not on this worksheet. The worksheet is deliberately kept generic so you can adjust it to your own unique needs.

For those expense categories where you really don't have a clue what the cost will be, guess. That's right. It is okay not to be perfect and it is also more valuable to keep moving through this exercise than to use the missing information as a reason to stop or get discouraged. You are already going through the most important process by thinking about these expenses and filling in most of the information. You can always add to this section later as new or more accurate information becomes available.

ADDITIONAL NOTES ABOUT THE CATEGORIES

This worksheet is a guideline for you. You may find you have to add or cross out and replace certain categories. Remember to do whatever works best for your unique financial picture.

This section will be especially helpful if you are on a very tight budget this year. Some of your expenses like insurance or taxes will be fixed and there will be no room for negotiating or eliminating this expense.

On the other hand, a number of the expenses may not be so immediate nor be considered "needs," but are still preferred when the extra money is available. When you have the whole picture in front of you and see the total cost it will be easier to make decisions about how to handle those expenses when the money is still tight.

Be sure to review the Suggestion List following these instructions so you can fully take advantage of this worksheet and include all the valuable information that belongs here. Below are a few notes for some of the categories.

Home/yard maintenance. This can include expenses that range from a new mattress to an addition to the house or backyard. If you have been thinking about new furniture and have been trying to decide when you can afford it, use this Yearly Budget Worksheet for your planning.

Auto expenses. If you stop to think this area through ahead of time, you can estimate when you might need tires or need to take your car in for its 60,000-mile checkup. This also would naturally include oil changes.

Medical expenses. These are often difficult to know in advance, yet it is helpful to think about the different areas on the Suggestion List ahead of time so you can anticipate a possible expense rather than react to it. Put some estimate down, even the small copays, to remind you of the expenses throughout the year.

Vacations. Plan your vacations in advance. Keep in mind the mini-weekend trip as well as those holiday family visits and summer vacations. Both gifts and vacations are good practice places for learning to live within your income. You may enjoy buying expensive gifts or going on exotic vacations, but if this puts a hardship on your budget, you may have to reevaluate your priorities. Either spend less on these categories or less on some other categories.

Gifts. For some households, these are a minimal expense. Yet for others who place a high priority on gifts, the gift expense area can be a major expense when remembering Christmas, birthdays (including the party expenses), weddings, Mother's and Father's Days, anniversaries, baby showers, graduation, etc. Planning out all this information ahead of time will make it all more manageable.

The Gift Giving Worksheet is a separate worksheet to use for outlining all the gifts you plan to give throughout the year. You can total the amounts for each month and transfer those totals to the "Gift" category on this worksheet. Even though Christmas gifts are often purchased throughout the year, I do suggest putting the whole Christmas gift expense total under December only to keep this planning simple.

Holiday events. This expense will vary from household to household depending on how you celebrate Valentine's Day, July 4th, Halloween, Thanksgiving, and other traditional and religious events in your family. Don't forget the cost of decorating the house or purchasing a new Halloween costume along with all the other related expenses. By listing these estimates as well as the others on this page, you will have a more realistic approach to all your upcoming expenses.

The **Christmas/Holiday Expense Worksheet** can help you fine-tune the real expense of the Christmas and holiday season on top of the gift expense. Many of my clients will guess an amount for this category. Then when we work through the real estimate with the worksheet, the total amount is usually three times their guess.

I started using your book when it got to the point where we just didn't know where all the money was going. I figured most of it was going to meals out, which turned out to be true, but what shocked me was the amount being spent on gifts!

All of these various expenses are just more examples of "where the money goes."

HOW TO USE THIS INFORMATION

Once you have taken time to estimate and project your upcoming nonmonthly expenses, you have valuable information that graphically shows you which months will be light and which ones will be difficult to deal with. At this point you can evaluate each expense and consider your choices: you can cut back, postpone, modify, or eliminate the expense. Which choice best fits your personal needs?

When you total all of these expenses, you can quickly see why there never seems to be enough money. This is where the Reserve Savings Account mentioned earlier in the How to Use *The Budget Kit* section now makes more sense. When you total these expenses and divide by 12 (to get your monthly average), you can see how much money must be put aside each month to prepare for these upcoming expenses. You then can transfer this amount onto the **Monthly Budget Worksheet** and list it as Reserve Savings to help you plan ahead for the month.

As you look at this completed worksheet, what does it tell you? First, as mentioned above, you can see which months are going to be high-stress months and which ones will be manageable light months. Now you have a guideline to let you know which month would be better for taking on additional expenses.

Second, you can see what you ideally need to put aside each month to save for all these expenses. If that amount is too much at this time, pick some of the fixed and most expensive categories, like property tax, gifts, auto repairs, etc., and start putting aside one-twelfth of those totals. You also can use the Goals Saving Record in Part One or the general Savings Activity Record in Part Three to help track your savings.

Third, and most significantly, that monthly average amount is how much you are "affected" indirectly each month by these expenses. This effect or impact usually shows up in the form of added credit card debt, more or larger loans, financial juggling, doing without, and overall frustration.

Now that you can see this and realize what has been happening to your overall budget each year, you can do something about it. That's the exciting part. As one woman said, "I'm depressed and excited at the same time!"

REMINDER

This worksheet is your guideline and is meant to be as flexible as possible. You are the one who decides how to utilize the worksheet and the information to your best advantage.

SUGGESTION LIST—
ADDITIONAL NONMONTHLY EXPENSES

You can either complete this information here and then transfer it to the Yearly Budget Worksheet or use this as your guideline as you fill in the worksheet directly from these ideas.

Some of the expenses listed may be a monthly expense for you. If so, enter those expenses on the Monthly Budget Worksheet, not here. The focus of the Yearly Budget Worksheet is only on the periodic, quarterly, semiannual, annual, and nonmonthly expenses.

	Description	Amount(s)	Months Due
Housing	Property Taxes		
	Homeowners Insurance/Renter's Insurance		
	Association/Condo Dues		
	Storage/Garage		
	Yard/Garden Supplies		
	Yard Service/Maintenance		
	Pool Chemicals/Maintenance		
	Pest/Termite Control		
	Security System		
	Home Improvement Projects		
	Home Repairs/Maintenance		
	Carpet Cleaning/Window Cleaning		
	Dry Cleaning (drapes, bedding)		
	Home Furnishings/Decorating		
	Furniture/Appliances/Electronic Equipment		
	Maintenance Agreements		
	Other _____		
Utilities (Nonmonthly)	Fuel/Propane		
	Firewood		
	Waste Management		
	Water/Water Softener		
	Other _____		
Transportation	Vehicle #1 Insurance		
	Vehicle #2 Insurance		
	Boat/RV/Motorcycle Insurance & Expenses		
	Emission Inspection		
	License Renewal/Registration		
	Oil Change/Tune-up		
	Other Maintenance and Repairs		
	Other _____		
Health	Other Insurance		
	Medical Exams/Lab Tests		
	Visits (Sick kids, allergy, etc.)		
	Physical Exam/School Physical		
	Prescriptions		
	Chiropractor		
	Dermatologist		
	Dental Exams/X-rays/Cleanings		
	Dental Work Needed		
	Orthodontia		
	Vision Exam/Glasses/Contacts		
	Alternative Health Practitioners		
	Vitamins/Supplements/Homeopathic		
	Other _____		

Description	Amount(s)	Months Due

Insurance (Other)
- Life Insurance
- Disability Insurance
- Other _____

Memberships
- Church/Temple
- Country Club
- Credit Card Annual Fees
- Gym Annual Fees
- Organizations/Clubs
- Professional Dues/License
- Auto Club
- Sports
- Warehouse Clubs
- Other _____

Computer
- Hardware/Software
- Upgrades
- Service/Maintenance
- Classes/Training

Education (Adult)
- Tuition
- Book/Supply Expenses
- Trade Journals/Magazines/Newspapers
- Workshops/Seminars/Speakers
- Other _____

Clothing (Adults and Children)
- Work Clothes/Uniforms/Shoes
- Seasonal Clothes/Shoes/Jackets
- Sports Clothes/Special Events
- Dry Cleaning/Alterations/Shoe Repair

Recreation (Adults)
- Parties
- Concerts/Sports Events/Season Tickets
- Fees: Permits/Tournament/League
- Hobbies/Sports Equipment and Maintenance
- Lessons
- Other _____

Vacation/Trips
- Transportation
- Lodging/Meals/Snacks
- Sights/Activities/Theatre/Galleries
- Shopping/Souvenirs/Film & Processing

Children
- Tuition/College Expenses
- School Supplies
- Photos/Yearbooks/Class Ring/Letter Jacket
- Prom/Homecoming (flowers, hair, dinner, etc.)
- Field Trips/Contests/Expos/Fund-Raising
- Camp Registration/Supplies
- Sports Equipment/Fees/Clinics
- Music Lessons/Equipment/Recitals/Costumes
- Other _____

Pets
- Pet Food
- Grooming/Pet Hotel
- Vet Expense/Shots/Rx/Dental
- Training/License

Misc.
- Donations
- Tax Preparation
- Taxes Due/Estimated Taxes
- Retirement Savings (IRA)

(Nonmonthly Anticipated Expenses)

FIXED AND ESTIMATED NONMONTHLY EXPENSES

		JAN.	FEB.	MAR.	APR.	MAY	JUNE	JULY	AUG.	SEPT.	OCT.	NOV.	DEC.	TOTAL	MO. AVG.
Housing	Property Tax/ Homeowners Insurance														
	Home/Yard Maintenance			Door 250	Yard 150		Drapes 250							650	54
	Utilities Sewer			65			20			50			85	220	18
Transportation	Auto Insurance Van Car			500 425						500 425				1,000 850	154
	Auto Expenses		Lube 25	Tires 250		Lube 25			Lube 25	Lic. 100	Lic. 80	Tune-up 150		655	55
Health	Insurance— Other Life		80			80			80			80		320	27
	Medical Expenses	Rx 75		250		Dr. A 20			Rx 75			Lab 70		490	41
	Dental/Vision Expenses		Dental 750					Vis. 300	Dental 75					1,125	94
Additional Nonmonthly Expenses	Dues/Fees /Taxes		Prof. Lic. 95		Tax Prep 300		Fish. 35	AAA 35	License 130			AMEX 55		650	54
	Education/Student Tuition Loan		85	Seminar 150		85			85	Seminar 100	85			590	49
	Clothing- Child Shoes/Coat	320				350			400					1,070	89
	Recreation	Concert 60				Fish Lic. 35				Season Ticket 75				170	14
	Vacation/Trips		Ski 250				800					300		1,350	112
	Magazines		YM 16			Kip 20						BL 39		75	6
	Gifts—Birthday	25	15	50			15	100		100	75			380	32
	Gifts—Other	Anniv. 40			Grad. 60	M. Day 50	F. Day 30		Shower 35		Wedding 40		Xmas 700	955	80
	Holiday Events				Easter 25			40			Halloween 60	TG 70	Xmas 400	595	50
	Children's Activities	65			Field Trip 100		Camp 150	Lessons 65		School 75	Photos 50			505	42
	Pets														
	Donations	15		WWF 25					G.P. 30		RC 50	CRS 100		220	18
	Personal	Perm 80			25				Perm 80		25			210	18
	Total	680	1,316	1,965	600	725	1,350	600	905	1,225	505	885	1,324	12,080	1,007

Reserve Savings: **Total Expenses $** __12,080__ **÷ 12 = $** __1,006.67__ **/Month** Rounded Up

YEARLY BUDGET WORKSHEET

(Nonmonthly Anticipated Expenses)

YEAR 20___

FIXED AND ESTIMATED NONMONTHLY EXPENSES

		JAN.	FEB.	MAR.	APR.	MAY	JUNE	JULY	AUG.	SEPT.	OCT.	NOV.	DEC.	TOTAL	MO. AVG.
Housing	Property Tax/Homeowners Insurance														
	Home/Yard Maintenance														
	Utilities														
Transportation	Auto Insurance														
	Auto Expenses														
Health	Insurance—Other														
	Medical Expenses														
	Dental/Vision Expenses														
Additional Nonmonthly Expenses	Dues/Fees														
	Education/Tuition														
	Clothing														
	Recreation														
	Vacation/Trips														
	Gifts—Birthday														
	Gifts—Other														
	Holiday Events														
	Children's Activities														
	Pets														
	Total														

Reserve Savings: Total Expenses $_____ ÷ 12 = $_____ /Month

Gift Giving Worksheet

Gift giving is often one of the most underestimated and overlooked budget categories in many households. People often are amazed, once they start recording all their expenses, just how much money actually is spent on gifts. It is not uncommon to forget occasional events or extended family members or teachers, bosses, hairdressers, and pets on this gift list when trying to estimate the overall gift budget.

This Gift Giving Worksheet works as a reminder as you anticipate the total yearly cost for all upcoming events involving gifts. Remembering Christmas and birthdays generally is easy. Events such as Father's

GIFT GIVING WORKSHEET

	Name	Amount: Christmas/ Hanukkah	Birthday	(Month Due)	Other Events*	Amount	(Month Due)
Parents							
Children							
Sisters/Brothers							

*Other: Anniversaries, weddings, showers, babies, Mother's Day, Father's Day, graduation, Bar Mitzvahs, religious events

Day or your parents' anniversary, however, often are overlooked until the month they occur. Even if you don't buy gifts but send flowers or go out to dinner instead, include these costs in your plan. By outlining all the members of your family and your friends and all the events celebrated in your household on this worksheet, and how much you want to budget for each, you have a handy total picture of what gift expenses to expect. You then can transfer these amounts to the "Gifts" section of the Yearly Budget Worksheet under the appropriate months.

As you think of gift ideas, you could add them in small print to this form as well.

GIFT GIVING WORKSHEET

	Name	Amount: Christmas/ Hanukkah	Birthday	(Month Due)	Other Events*	Amount	(Month Due)
Friends/Other							
Grandparents							
Aunts/Uncles							
Nieces/Nephews							
Children's Friends							

*Other: Anniversaries, weddings, showers, babies, Mother's Day, Father's Day, graduation, Bar Mitzvahs, religious events

CHRISTMAS/HOLIDAY EXPENSE WORKSHEET

Item	Estimate	Already Have	Actual Cost
Tree/Wreath			
Lights—House/Tree			
Baked Goods/Ginger House			
Parties/Food/Liquor Host Gifts			
Poinsettias/Candles Decorations/Crafts			
Gift Wrap Greeting Cards			
Postage Shipping/Boxes			
Film Processing Family Portraits			
Clothes/Shoes/Jewelry			
Meals Out			
Movies/Ballet/Plays/Galleries Travel/Tour			
Workplace Events			
Donations			
Batteries/Misc. (Gifts) Other			
Total Amount			

SOURCE OF MONEY FOR GIFTS AND HOLIDAY EXPENSES

Total Amount for Gifts:
(See Gift Giving Worksheet) $ _____

Total Amount—Expenses:
(See Worksheet at Left) $ _____

TOTAL AMOUNT NEEDED: $ _____

How much is available from the following sources to cover these expenses:

Source	Amount	Notes
Current Income		
Extra Hours/ Part-time Job		
Savings Account(s)		
Gift Money/ Bonus		
Put on Charge Cards		
Borrow		
Total Amount		

Monthly Budget Worksheet

WHY A MONTHLY BUDGET WORKSHEET?

The Monthly Budget Worksheet is designed to provide a guideline for coordinating your monthly bills and expenses with your *take-home* pay. Your monthly bills are often easier to remember because most bills come in the mail. Forgotten, however, are the expenses each month such as meals eaten out, haircuts, gifts, books, tapes, seminars, and the like that often throw off the monthly budget.

This worksheet is especially helpful during those lean times when work hours are reduced and the amount of bills to pay exceeds the money coming in. This guideline will give you a better overall picture of your monthly obligations and lifestyle expenses. The categories are kept general to allow for flexibility and necessary additions based on your own personal financial needs.

Often something as simple as this worksheet can be the difference between financial chaos and financial control. For the Mathews the true test came when the commission check was exceptionally low one month. After months of working diligently on their budget, this young, ambitious couple had the skills and tools to tighten up and be creative about their spending. They knew what to do. Banana bread was made at home to replace the sales meeting bagels, all meals out were eliminated, brown bag meals and soggy sandwiches replaced the business meals out while on the road, and all other discretionary spending was cut back. By the end of the month the Mathews were ecstatic as they made it through the month financially intact—all the bills were paid, good meals were eaten at home, no credit card charges, no little loans, and, best of all, they felt totally motivated by their ability to take control of the situation.

HOW TO GET STARTED

To use the Monthly Budget Worksheet, look at the filled in sample on page 35. Start with the top row next to "Income Source" and indicate in each column where your money is coming from for that month, whether it is from your job, your spouse's job, your checkbook balance rolled over from the previous month, investment or rental income, savings, a refund, etc.

Next, on the second row next to "Net Income Total ① Amount" near the top in each column write down the *net amount* of each paycheck or other money that will be used to pay for those monthly expenses. How many columns you fill in depends on how often you are paid each month. Of course, there are many job situations where the amount may vary or is not always known, such as with commission sales. If this is the case, make a very *conservative* estimate until the actual amount is known. If your income is very erratic, you also can work with the **Variable Income Worksheet** following this section.

You will notice the emphasis on net income and not on gross income throughout the workbook. This way, you are dealing only with the cash you actually have for paying your bills. Your payroll deductions and taxes are not being ignored. You can record that information on the **Monthly Expense Record** as well as on the End-of-the-Year Tax Information form on page 103.

On the third row under the "Income Source" amount ② there is room to add the date each paycheck is received. This will help with your planning when working around due dates and paying your bills.

Finally, total all of the income and other sources of money across the top row and put that total in the column next to "Total Income" at the bottom left side of ⑤ the page.

WHAT MAKES THIS WORKSHEET UNIQUE

Now let's look at all those bills. Under the column ③ "Amount" is where you will list every bill and expense you can think of that will be coming up for that particular month. Included will be the obvious bills as well as the incidental, like planning to buy a new suit, developing rolls of film, or having someone service your computer that month. This is not necessarily an *average* monthly budget that is being developed. And although it may well turn out to be an average monthly budget, the real purpose here is to take time to outline the specific month coming up and look at all of its unique expenses beyond the average amounts. For example, if your relatives are coming to visit for a week during the month you are planning, your grocery, meals out, utility, gasoline, and entertainment amounts may all be higher than usual that month.

This approach is what makes this budgeting process more unique than the standard method of taking the yearly total of expenses and dividing it by 12 months for a monthly average.

The other unique feature is learning how to coordinate the timing of the income with the due dates and needs of the expenses using this worksheet. I have had numerous clients finally "get it" when they saw how to work the payments and general expenses according to the timing of the income. *They no longer had to try to pay all their bills with the first paycheck out of fear of running out of money and then figure out how to live the next week with no money until they were paid again.*

Other clients used this worksheet to determine ahead of time how much cash to pull out for each week for various cash expenses and eliminated all the incidental nonplanned runs to the ATM machine.

This worksheet will definitely help you become proactive and more relaxed in your approach to managing money instead of staying in a reactive mode.

So now let's review how to fill in the expenses in the column under the "Amount" heading. The Sample page will help you get a better idea.

PAY YOURSELF FIRST

Notice that "Allowance/Mad Money" and "Sav- ④ ings" are under "Fixed Amounts." The phrase "pay yourself first" has been said many times. It is a valid statement and a very important rule because if you penny-pinch to the point where there is no money left for "Allowance/Mad Money," you will end up bickering, frustrated, and disappointed with the whole budget idea. The "Allowance/Mad Money" should be yours to do with as you please. Decide how much "Allowance/Mad Money" each member needs to allow for little splurges and yet not ignore the necessary expenses.

Just as important under "Fixed Amounts" is "Savings." Again, this is paying yourself first. Consider "Savings" as an *expense,* setting aside a specific amount or percentage of your check at the same time you are completing the other categories of the worksheet. In this manner, you will be thinking of "Savings" as an expense so that it is planned for regularly and not dependent on leftover funds.

Remember the different savings accounts—**reserve** (for upcoming known bills and expenses listed on the **Yearly Budget Worksheet**), **emergency** (equivalent to three months of take-home pay for unknown disasters), and **goals** (wish list)—and try to save regularly for them. See the Savings Activity Record on page 120 for tracking your savings.

Once you have saved enough money for the reserve and emergency accounts, you will realize that it is actually possible to save money. Saving for your goals soon becomes more exciting and challenging as you realize that reaching your goals now is possible.

NOW FOR SOME PRACTICE AT BUDGETING

In many cases, such as utilities or other areas under "Fixed Variable" and "Occasional," the exact amount of the bill is unknown. For those categories, this is where your budgeting practice comes in as you estimate the bills until the exact amount is known. Remember to keep in mind those other expenses that are not seen as bills but show up on a daily basis: groceries, gas, entertainment, clothing, etc. Those must be planned for as well. Here you will take an estimated guess (budget) as to what you will need and the amount you can spend. If you use the **Monthly Expense Record** starting on page 74 for tracking your expenses each month, you will have a better sense of some averages to use for these categories when estimating. Once you become familiar with estimating your expenditures, you will successfully begin to live within your budget. If your budget is realistic, you soon will choose to do without certain unnecessary items to remain within the projected budget.

MORE MONTH THAN MONEY— NOW WHAT?

Before you total the "Amount" column, think again if there is anything else that may be coming up as an expense for the particular month you are outlining. Look at the categories on the **Monthly Expense Record** and the **Suggestion List—Additional Non-monthly Expenses** in the **Yearly Budget Worksheet** section and see if any ideas are triggered for possible expenses. And finally, look at the Yearly Budget Worksheet. If you have not put the 1/12th into reserve savings, did you include those unique expenses when planning for this particular month?

⑤ Now it's time to tally up and face the total. Put that total figure for this column "Amount" at the bottom next to "Total Expenses." As you filled in this column you probably were already telling yourself this is more than you have coming in. If that is the case, at least now you can see it in black and white and know why some of the months have been running short and why those expenses probably ended up on the credit cards.

Remember, *this worksheet is done before the month ever begins.* It is a projection of your anticipated budget. That means you now have the time and opportunity to take charge and do something about this information. You always have the following choices: postpone, cut back, eliminate, or find creative alternatives.

Contact the creditors and see what special arrangements you can make. Many will accommodate you and allow postponed or partial payments if you notify them. What can you eliminate? Lattes, books, CDs, meals out, full-price movies, clothes, and gadgets are starters. Go through and reevaluate each expense.

What else can you do? How can you bring more money in? Can you get more overtime hours or a part-time job? Do you have enough "stuff" to have a yard sale? What if you took your unused books, CDs, and clothes to the resale shops for some extra cash?

In the meantime, possibly you have been building a small emergency fund and can cover expenses this time by withdrawing the necessary amount. This should be an absolute last resort, however, with cutbacks planned for the next few months so that you can replenish your emergency fund once again.

TIMING INCOME WITH PAYMENTS AND EXPENSES

Now that you have reworked your numbers so your expenses match your income, go back to the fixed expenses at the top under the "Amount" column and distribute and balance the more expensive bills over the different pay periods in each column based on due dates and income dates. Write in these figures under the "Income" column. If some pay periods, like the beginning of the month, are pretty top heavy with bills, try contacting the creditor and see about arranging to change the date according to your next paycheck for future payments.

Another method is to allocate small portions from some or all of the paychecks to cover a large bill, such as the mortgage. What some readers have done in those cases is to itemize a portion under different pay periods and then write a check for that amount and keep it in the envelope until the final check and full amount is ready. They then sent the envelope with the multiple checks totaling the complete payment.

Categories like groceries, gasoline, and meals out are generally divided somewhat under each pay period. You decide how best to balance all the expenses under each of the "Income" columns. Working with pencil will again be preferred, as it may take some fine-tuning to balance each of the "Income" columns with the expenses.

GETTING CONTROL OF YOUR FINANCES

You have just completed an important step in getting and keeping control of your finances. Of course, doing a Monthly Budget Worksheet does not change or increase the amount of actual money earned. Being aware, however, of where and how the money is spent will give you the feeling that you are beginning to control your money and will help you stretch the use of those dollars more than ever before.

Happy budgeting!

I was shocked into action when I worked out my budget on the Monthly Budget Worksheet and realized I was $1,000 short. Now after four years all our bills are paid in full and we are completely out of debt. Without putting information down on paper every month I don't think I could have done it.

MONTHLY BUDGET WORKSHEET

INCOME SOURCE:		Chris	Kim	Chris	Kim	Reserve Savings
① Net Income Total Amount:		896	1,407	880	1,407	1,380
Expenses	③ Amount	Date: ② 9/4	9/7	9/18	9/21	9/15

Fixed Amounts

Expenses	Amount	Chris 9/4	Kim 9/7	Chris 9/18	Kim 9/21	Reserve Savings 9/15
Mortgage/Rent	784	784				
Car Payments	291			291		
Other Loans student	167			167		
Internet Access						
Day Care						
Insurance Auto	500*					500
Auto	425*					425
Clubs/Dues						
Emergency	215				115	
Goals	75		100		75	
Savings Reserve	1,007		400	300	307	
④ Allowance/Mad Money	50	20		30		

Fixed Variable

Expenses	Amount	Chris 9/4	Kim 9/7	Chris 9/18	Kim 9/21	Reserve Savings 9/15
Electricity	75			75		
Oil/Gas	45			45		
Water/Garbage	125*					125
Telephone/Cell Phone	65			65		
Cable TV/Satellite	35			35		
Groceries	450	50	150	50	200	
Meals Out	125		30	50	45	
Auto Expense/Gas	85		30	30	25	
Auto License	100*					100
Activities	30					
Child Allowance	40	10	10	10	40	
Church/Charity	325		70		255	

Occasional

Expenses	Amount	Chris 9/4	Kim 9/7	Chris 9/18	Kim 9/21	Reserve Savings 9/15
Household Photos	20			20		
Personal Perm	80*					80
Clothes /Dry Cleaning	75 / 35	25	35		50	
Medical Prescrip.	35		35			
Child Expense School Exp.	75*					75
Recreation Season Ticket	75*					75
Counseling	130		65		65	
Books, CDs	35	10		25		

Installment

Expenses	Amount	Chris 9/4	Kim 9/7	Chris 9/18	Kim 9/21	Reserve Savings 9/15
Credit Cards Movies/Videos	55		25		30	
Visa	100			100		
MC	200				200	

Total

Expenses	Amount	Chris 9/4	Kim 9/7	Chris 9/18	Kim 9/21	Reserve Savings 9/15
⑤ **Total Income**	4,590					
Total Expense Excludes*	4,549	899	1,408	835	1,407	1,380
Total Excess	41			45		
Total Short		−3	−1			

*Paid from Reserve Savings (Yearly Budget Worksheet) and not included in this Total Expense figure.

MONTHLY BUDGET WORKSHEET

	INCOME SOURCE:						
	Net Income Total Amount:						
	Expenses	**Amount**	**Date:**				
Fixed Amounts	Mortgage/Rent						
	Car Payments						
	Other Loans						
	Internet Access						
	Day Care						
	Insurance						
	Clubs/Dues						
	Savings						
	Allowance/Mad Money						
Fixed Variable	Electricity						
	Oil/Gas						
	Water/Garbage						
	Telephone/Cell Phone						
	Cable TV/Satellite						
	Groceries						
	Meals Out						
	Auto Expense/Gas						
	Church/Charity						
Occasional	Household						
	Personal						
	Clothes						
	Medical						
	Child Expense						
	Recreation						
Installment	Credit Cards						
Total	**Total Income**						
	Total Expense						
	Total Excess						
	Total Short						

MONTHLY BUDGET WORKSHEET

FEBRUARY

INCOME SOURCE:						
Net Income Total Amount:						

	Expenses	Amount	Date:				
Fixed Amounts	Mortgage/Rent						
	Car Payments						
	Other Loans						
	Internet Access						
	Day Care						
	Insurance						
	Clubs/Dues						
	Savings						
	Allowance/Mad Money						
Fixed Variable	Electricity						
	Oil/Gas						
	Water/Garbage						
	Telephone/Cell Phone						
	Cable TV/Satellite						
	Groceries						
	Meals Out						
	Auto Expense/Gas						
	Church/Charity						
Occasional	Household						
	Personal						
	Clothes						
	Medical						
	Child Expense						
	Recreation						
Installment	Credit Cards						
Total	Total Income						
	Total Expense						
	Total Excess						
	Total Short						

MONTHLY BUDGET WORKSHEET

MARCH

INCOME SOURCE:							
Net Income Total Amount:							

	Expenses	Amount	Date:				
Fixed Amounts	Mortgage/Rent						
	Car Payments						
	Other Loans						
	Internet Access						
	Day Care						
	Insurance						
	Clubs/Dues						
	Savings						
	Allowance/Mad Money						
Fixed Variable	Electricity						
	Oil/Gas						
	Water/Garbage						
	Telephone/Cell Phone						
	Cable TV/Satellite						
	Groceries						
	Meals Out						
	Auto Expense/Gas						
	Church/Charity						
Occasional	Household						
	Personal						
	Clothes						
	Medical						
	Child Expense						
	Recreation						
Installment	Credit Cards						
Total	Total Income						
	Total Expense						
	Total Excess						
	Total Short						

MONTHLY BUDGET WORKSHEET

INCOME SOURCE:						
Net Income Total Amount:						
Expenses	**Amount**	**Date:**				
Mortgage/Rent						
Car Payments						
Other Loans						
Internet Access						
Day Care						
Insurance						
Clubs/Dues						
Savings						
Allowance/Mad Money						
Electricity						
Oil/Gas						
Water/Garbage						
Telephone/Cell Phone						
Cable TV/Satellite						
Groceries						
Meals Out						
Auto Expense/Gas						
Church/Charity						
Household						
Personal						
Clothes						
Medical						
Child Expense						
Recreation						
Credit Cards						
Total Income						
Total Expense						
Total Excess						
Total Short						

Row groups (left margin labels): Fixed Amounts, Fixed Variable, Occasional, Installment, Total

MONTHLY BUDGET WORKSHEET

INCOME SOURCE:						
Net Income Total Amount:						

	Expenses	Amount	Date:			
Fixed Amounts	Mortgage/Rent					
	Car Payments					
	Other Loans					
	Internet Access					
	Day Care					
	Insurance					
	Clubs/Dues					
	Savings					
	Allowance/Mad Money					
Fixed Variable	Electricity					
	Oil/Gas					
	Water/Garbage					
	Telephone/Cell Phone					
	Cable TV/Satellite					
	Groceries					
	Meals Out					
	Auto Expense/Gas					
	Church/Charity					
Occasional	Household					
	Personal					
	Clothes					
	Medical					
	Child Expense					
	Recreation					
Installment	Credit Cards					
Total	Total Income					
	Total Expense					
	Total Excess					
	Total Short					

MONTHLY BUDGET WORKSHEET

	Expenses	Amount	Date:				
INCOME SOURCE:							
Net Income Total Amount:							
Fixed Amounts	Mortgage/Rent						
	Car Payments						
	Other Loans						
	Internet Access						
	Day Care						
	Insurance						
	Clubs/Dues						
	Savings						
	Allowance/Mad Money						
Fixed Variable	Electricity						
	Oil/Gas						
	Water/Garbage						
	Telephone/Cell Phone						
	Cable TV/Satellite						
	Groceries						
	Meals Out						
	Auto Expense/Gas						
	Church/Charity						
Occasional	Household						
	Personal						
	Clothes						
	Medical						
	Child Expense						
	Recreation						
Installment	Credit Cards						
Total	Total Income						
	Total Expense						
	Total Excess						
	Total Short						

MONTHLY BUDGET WORKSHEET

	INCOME SOURCE:						
	Net Income Total Amount:						
	Expenses	**Amount**	**Date:**				
Fixed Amounts	Mortgage/Rent						
	Car Payments						
	Other Loans						
	Internet Access						
	Day Care						
	Insurance						
	Clubs/Dues						
	Savings						
	Allowance/Mad Money						
Fixed Variable	Electricity						
	Oil/Gas						
	Water/Garbage						
	Telephone/Cell Phone						
	Cable TV/Satellite						
	Groceries						
	Meals Out						
	Auto Expense/Gas						
	Church/Charity						
Occasional	Household						
	Personal						
	Clothes						
	Medical						
	Child Expense						
	Recreation						
Installment	Credit Cards						
Total	**Total Income**						
	Total Expense						
	Total Excess						
	Total Short						

MONTHLY BUDGET WORKSHEET

INCOME SOURCE:						
Net Income Total Amount:						

	Expenses	**Amount**	**Date:**				
Fixed Amounts	Mortgage/Rent						
	Car Payments						
	Other Loans						
	Internet Access						
	Day Care						
	Insurance						
	Clubs/Dues						
	Savings						
	Allowance/Mad Money						
Fixed Variable	Electricity						
	Oil/Gas						
	Water/Garbage						
	Telephone/Cell Phone						
	Cable TV/Satellite						
	Groceries						
	Meals Out						
	Auto Expense/Gas						
	Church/Charity						
Occasional	Household						
	Personal						
	Clothes						
	Medical						
	Child Expense						
	Recreation						
Installment	Credit Cards						
Total	**Total Income**						
	Total Expense						
	Total Excess						
	Total Short						

MONTHLY BUDGET WORKSHEET

INCOME SOURCE:						
Net Income Total Amount:						

	Expenses	**Amount**	**Date:**				
Fixed Amounts	Mortgage/Rent						
	Car Payments						
	Other Loans						
	Internet Access						
	Day Care						
	Insurance						
	Clubs/Dues						
	Savings						
	Allowance/Mad Money						
Fixed Variable	Electricity						
	Oil/Gas						
	Water/Garbage						
	Telephone/Cell Phone						
	Cable TV/Satellite						
	Groceries						
	Meals Out						
	Auto Expense/Gas						
	Church/Charity						
Occasional	Household						
	Personal						
	Clothes						
	Medical						
	Child Expense						
	Recreation						
Installment	Credit Cards						
Total	**Total Income**						
	Total Expense						
	Total Excess						
	Total Short						

INCOME SOURCE:						
Net Income Total Amount:						

	Expenses	Amount	Date:				
Fixed Amounts	Mortgage/Rent						
	Car Payments						
	Other Loans						
	Internet Access						
	Day Care						
	Insurance						
	Clubs/Dues						
	Savings						
	Allowance/Mad Money						
Fixed Variable	Electricity						
	Oil/Gas						
	Water/Garbage						
	Telephone/Cell Phone						
	Cable TV/Satellite						
	Groceries						
	Meals Out						
	Auto Expense/Gas						
	Church/Charity						
Occasional	Household						
	Personal						
	Clothes						
	Medical						
	Child Expense						
	Recreation						
Installment	Credit Cards						
Total	**Total Income**						
	Total Expense						
	Total Excess						
	Total Short						

MONTHLY BUDGET WORKSHEET

INCOME SOURCE:						
Net Income Total Amount:						

	Expenses	Amount	Date:				
Fixed Amounts	Mortgage/Rent						
	Car Payments						
	Other Loans						
	Internet Access						
	Day Care						
	Insurance						
	Clubs/Dues						
	Savings						
	Allowance/Mad Money						
Fixed Variable	Electricity						
	Oil/Gas						
	Water/Garbage						
	Telephone/Cell Phone						
	Cable TV/Satellite						
	Groceries						
	Meals Out						
	Auto Expense/Gas						
	Church/Charity						
Occasional	Household						
	Personal						
	Clothes						
	Medical						
	Child Expense						
	Recreation						
Installment	Credit Cards						
Total	**Total Income**						
	Total Expense						
	Total Excess						
	Total Short						

MONTHLY BUDGET WORKSHEET

INCOME SOURCE:						
Net Income Total Amount:						

	Expenses	Amount	Date:				
Fixed Amounts	Mortgage/Rent						
	Car Payments						
	Other Loans						
	Internet Access						
	Day Care						
	Insurance						
	Clubs/Dues						
	Savings						
	Allowance/Mad Money						
Fixed Variable	Electricity						
	Oil/Gas						
	Water/Garbage						
	Telephone/Cell Phone						
	Cable TV/Satellite						
	Groceries						
	Meals Out						
	Auto Expense/Gas						
	Church/Charity						
Occasional	Household						
	Personal						
	Clothes						
	Medical						
	Child Expense						
	Recreation						
Installment	Credit Cards						
Total	Total Income						
	Total Expense						
	Total Excess						
	Total Short						

Variable Income Worksheet

Planning your monthly finances can be especially challenging when your income is not predictable or regular each month. Often I hear people say they cannot create a budget because their income is based on commissions, self-employment, or other irregular income and therefore they feel they have no way to plan ahead. Actually, having a spending plan that gives you a clear outline of your basic monthly fixed expenses and a plan for covering them is even *more* important when your income is not regular.

I have met with many clients who have been in variable income situations, which is the reason I added this new worksheet. For many of those clients, utilizing all three of the main worksheets together—**Yearly Budget Worksheet, Monthly Budget Worksheet,** and **Monthly Expense Record** (found in this section of the workbook)—worked most effectively. They were able to get a handle on the best approach for dealing with those three-month stretches of no income and then successfully plan the best way to distribute the bonus check or commission or other business income when it did come in.

This worksheet is designed to give you a guideline for planning a system that helps you know and cover your basic fixed monthly expenses every month, whether you receive income or not. Without a clear long-range plan, it is very tempting to react to a large sum of money as a mini windfall. This worksheet will help you keep a big-picture perspective. You will learn to plan proactively and stay prepared for upcoming financial obligations by saving the appropriate amount of money.

The key is starting with a conservative approach and stashing as much of the income as possible into savings to act as your future monthly income. This is especially true if you do not really know when the next amount of money will be coming in or how much. You may only know that it is very likely that the case will be settled, or the sale will close, or the partnership may have enough to pay salaries again, or the company will be giving some bonus distribution at some point. And yes, there is always the possibility that something can happen and the money may *not* come through.

That's why you want contingency plans: money in the bank; ability to cut back dramatically with the spending; good credit rating to help with access to loans; back-up help from family or friends; other job possibilities; good relationships with all your creditors to work out short-term arrangements; attention to your investments to be sure they are performing well; and a reality check on the real cost of your cars and other personal property that you may want to sell or replace with less expensive versions.

As you work out the history or the current record of your irregular income, you may see that there actually is a pattern. With this pattern you can begin to coordinate some of your big-ticket payments, such as annual or semiannual insurances, tuition, or taxes, with the timing of the income. Clients have often been amazed to realize how much power they had over their finances once they were armed with information. Many times you can make arrangements for totally different payment dates and even payments if you have a clear outlined plan and you discuss it with a receptive customer service representative or supervisor for that company.

There may be many months when no money is coming in and you are living solely on the savings you have set aside specifically for those months. Continue to stay conscious of your spending and money patterns during this time. Even though living that way can be unsettling, remember to pat yourself on the back for having the foresight and prudence to put sufficient funds aside.

HOW TO USE THIS WORKSHEET

The purpose of the Variable Income Worksheet is twofold. First, it serves as a planner for projecting upcoming income to the best of your ability. Second, once the actual income comes in and you record this information, you will have a record to refer to next year when projecting the new year. I usually suggest you use pencil or have a way to easily change your numbers because this whole book is a *workbook* and your work is always in progress.

WINDFALL PLANNER

Before starting on this Variable Income Worksheet it may help to review the Windfall Planner worksheet on page 54. The Windfall Planner is helpful for those one-time lump sums of money, such as an insurance settlement, inheritance, or company bonus. Using that planner helps you to see the many options to consider and to then prioritize the distribution of those funds.

MULTIPLE SALES MONTHLY PLANNER

If you are in sales, before you begin this Variable Income Worksheet I want you to know about the Multiple Sales Monthly Planner on pages 56–58. As you know, variable commission income could be from multiple closings on products and projects as well as from one big commission check. To help itemize all those different possible closing amounts, I have added an accessory planner. With this planner, you will have a way to record those sales that are projected, listed, pending, or sold for each month. Once you have completed the total amount of actual closings, you can transfer that monthly total to the Variable Income Worksheet under "Income Source."

Income Source A variety of income sources are listed. If your source does not fit any of these categories, cross them out and insert your own. When you know the amount or approximate amount of the bonus, commission, or other income source and the month, enter that amount in the column under the appropriate month.

If you know the month but have no clue what the figure will be, like dividends or royalties, only that some amount will be coming in, place an "X" in the box under the month to remind you when some money will be arriving. This also acts as a reminder in the event some expected money has not arrived and you can then follow up on the delay.

Once that large check does arrive, the critical step is to evaluate how best to distribute those funds. What do you pay off first? How much do you save? How much do you need to live on for this month and possibly many more months? The following sections will help you determine the best ways to use the money, including how much money you will need, how much to put aside in savings, and how much debt you can pay off.

Estimated Taxes/Savings After you finish relishing the nice bonus package or commission check that just came in, remember that the very next step is addressing the taxes. If taxes have not been withdrawn from this particular source of income, then this is the place to start and make sure you calculate how much to put aside for taxes.

There are enough resources to advise you where the best place is for "parking" your money while saving it. You may already work with a tax accountant or financial planner who can advise you on where and how much to save. As a general guideline, I recommend putting aside approximately 25 to 30 percent as a minimum starting place for your basic commissions and other job income. The most important point is to do it. Move that money over to savings, a money market account, mutual fund, or whatever seems most appropriate right away so you are dealing with realistic numbers as you plan your budget. Some people find it easier to dedicate a separate savings account for taxes only so they are not tempted to use that money for other household expenses or emergencies.

The goal throughout this workbook is to help you to manage your finances proactively instead of reactively. Ignoring the tax issue or saying you will take more money out of the next check for taxes because this time you really need all the money, starts to set you up for that reactive crisis management cycle once again. This time you can change that cycle. Be patient and know you *can* turn things around. Outline this plan and follow it as closely as you can.

Note about Stock Options In this world of stock options and other huge money packages, it is more important than ever to pay attention to the tax consequences. It is not unusual to see more than 50 percent in the end going to taxes depending on your income bracket and other factors. I have witnessed a lot of financial havoc for clients who had not withdrawn enough for taxes. Large sums of money can easily draw you in emotionally and skew your good sense. Be sure to talk with a tax accountant for an accurate projection before buying that new car with cash.

Fixed and Variable Expenses The next step is addressing the Basic Monthly Household and Personal Expenses part of the worksheet. I recommend completing the Monthly Budget Worksheet starting on page 36 and the Monthly Expense Record starting on page 76 to help you use this section more efficiently. The design does allow planning from this form exclusively, however, the other worksheets are more comprehensive so there is less chance of overlooking any critical expenses.

If you have been using the Monthly Expense Record for *tracking* your daily spending, and have good records of all your fixed bills and general expenses, then those totals can easily be transferred to this worksheet. The Monthly Budget Worksheet allows more room for *projecting* your monthly plan of any upcoming bills and other unique expenses for the month.

Just a reminder, the Monthly Budget Worksheet is the beginning step if you don't have a history of expenses yet. This worksheet offers you a guideline to think about and project the many areas beyond the bills where money may be spent during each month.

Credit Cards Once the basic living expenses are handled, it is time to calculate how much to pay toward the credit card balances. In the ideal world, the only credit card balances would be those that are paid off each month. Until that time arrives, use this worksheet to pay off your credit card balances as quickly as possible and not waste another dime on finance charges, late fees, and over the limit fees. The Debt Payoff Record (starting on page 64) can help you ultimately get on top of the debt situation.

If planning to make payments on the credit card debt is particularly difficult one month because of the low income and high fixed expenses, still try to find some way to pay the minimum due plus an extra ten dollars on each of the credit cards. This small additional amount will save you substantially over the long run.

During those months when a large sum of money is received, take this opportunity to pay down or off some or all of your credit card debt. Of course, a lot depends on the overall plan, your future income, and your future needs. Find a balance in this plan so you pay off enough of the credit card bill to save you significant finance charges and yet have enough funds to be prepared for future months of no income.

Major Periodic Expenses The missing link in most budgets is the lack of planning for periodic ex-

penses that show up throughout the year as quarterly, annual, or periodic expenses but are not part of the monthly picture.

The Yearly Budget Worksheet on page 27 will help you determine what periodic expenses exist and which ones are imperative to pay. If you have not yet completed this section, go ahead and review pages 24 and 25 for a suggested list of expenses that may apply to your situation right now. Add these totals to the worksheet under the appropriate monthly column.

Deposit to or Withdraw from Savings Add your total income and total expenses under each month on this form. The idea here is to see how much money is left over or is short after taking care of all the basic needs outlined above. Once you can see that total amount in black and white, you can again take some constructive action. Depositing money into savings can be extremely satisfying after having a long stretch of debt and very little income.

For those surplus months, be sure to stash that excess money right away. If you have completed all the information for all months, it will be very apparent which months you will be needing to withdraw from savings to cover the expenses. The Windfall Planner on page 54 is another tool available for you in the event you unexpectedly receive a large sum of money.

There may still be situations where you can't predict when the next month will be a surplus or even an income month for you. In those cases, maximum savings is critical along with clear contingency plans as mentioned earlier. At some point, if this unpredictable income continues too long and erodes your savings, lifestyle, and personal well-being, you may want to re-evaluate your work options or even where you now live.

Remember, when you have knowledge, you have more power to make decisions. Use this section as your road map to a more powerful financial future.

It took us about seven months, but now we finally have a handle on our erratic income. There were times when we would go three months without any kind of income. In the beginning, it seemed like all we were doing was dodging phone calls and juggling promises. But then, by carefully tracking and planning our expenses over time and working closely with the creditors, we were able to work out how much we needed every month to run the household. When we finally did get paid we knew exactly what bills to pay, how much had to be covered, and what amount we needed to carry over into savings each time. What a difference this has made. We feel like we can breathe again!

VARIABLE INCOME WORKSHEET

Income Source	Jan.	Feb.	Mar.	Apr.	May	June	July	Aug.	Sep.	Oct.	Nov.	Dec.	Total
Investment Income _____ _____													
Commissions _____ _____													
Bonus _____ _____													
Business Income _____ _____													
Consultant _____ _____													
Reimbursement _____ _____													
Freelance _____ _____													
Royalty _____ _____													
Other* _____ _____ _____													
TOTAL INCOME													

*Tax refund, cash gifts, inheritance, trust, gratuities, rental property, insurance settlement, property sale, etc.

BASIC MONTHLY HOUSEHOLD AND PERSONAL EXPENSES
(Refer to Monthly Budget Worksheet and Yearly Budget Worksheet for more comprehensive categories.)

Expense	Jan.	Feb.	Mar.	Apr.	May	June
Estimated Taxes						
Fixed: Mortgage/Rent						
Car Payment/Lease						
Loans						
_____						
Insurance						
_____						
_____						
Variable: Utilities						
Phones						
Groceries						
Gasoline						
_____						
_____						
Credit Cards:						
_____						
_____						
_____						
Major Periodic Expenses: _____						
TOTAL EXPENSES						
Total Income						
Less Total Expenses						
Difference						
Deposit into Savings*						
Withdraw from Savings						

*If extra funds are available this month, see the Windfall Planner on page 54.

BASIC MONTHLY HOUSEHOLD AND PERSONAL EXPENSES
(Refer to Monthly Budget Worksheet and Yearly Budget Worksheet for more comprehensive categories.)

Expense	July	Aug.	Sept.	Oct.	Nov.	Dec.
Estimated Taxes						
Fixed: Mortgage/Rent						
Car Payment/Lease						
Loans						
_____						
Insurance						
_____						
_____						
Variable: Utilities						
Phones						
Groceries						
Gasoline						
_____						
_____						
Credit Cards: _____						
_____						
_____						
_____						
Major Periodic Expenses: _____						
TOTAL EXPENSES						
Total Income						
Less Total Expenses						
Difference						
Deposit into Savings*						
Withdraw from Savings						

*If extra funds are available this month, see the Windfall Planner on page 54.

Windfall Planner

Use this planner to outline a plan for prioritizing how you want to best utilize the money when you receive or are about to receive a large lump sum of money.

WINDFALL PLANNER

Date: _____

Source of Money: _____

Total Amount: _____

Possible Expense Items	Amount	or	Percent
Estimated Taxes to Put in Savings (If no taxes have been taken out.)	_____		_____
Catch Up on Payments Currently Behind	_____		_____
Back Taxes Still Due	_____		_____
Credit Card(s)—Pay Down or Off	_____		_____
Loan(s)—Pay Down or Off	_____		_____
Cover ___ No. of Months of Living Expenses (Put this in savings.)	_____		_____
Stock Up on Household and/or Grocery Items	_____		_____
Upcoming Major Expense(s) (See Yearly Budget Worksheet page 27.)	_____		_____
Reserve Savings Account (See Yearly Budget Worksheet page 27.)	_____		_____
Emergency Savings Acocunt	_____		_____
Home Improvement Project(s)	_____		_____
New Purchases	_____		_____
Investments/Retirement/College	_____		_____
Vacation/Travel/Trips	_____		_____
Other _____	_____		_____
_____	_____		_____
_____	_____		_____
GRAND TOTAL	$ _____		_____ %

Multiple Sales
Monthly Planner

Whether you are an interior decorator in a home furnishing store, a REALTOR®, or software salesperson, if your income is based on commission, this Multiple Sales Monthly Planner is designed to help you get a handle on those ongoing monthly sales activities.

The goal is to have one place to list all your projected, pending, and closing sales for each month and to keep the form open enough to allow for the many changes that occur throughout the month. This is another place it would be wise to use pencil.

Use this planner as an addendum to the forms you already use through your work and as a way to determine income totals for the month to use in the various worksheets in this workbook. This form is deliberately kept generic to address the unique needs of different sales environments.

You may need to alter code titles listed on the bottom of the planner, depending on the line of work you are in and, in some cases, they may not apply at all. The date as well as the amount for closing a sale or making a potential sale could be known or approximate; again, put down the information that works best for your needs.

Modify this planner as much as you need so it is a functional tool for you.

MULTIPLE SALES MONTHLY PLANNER

JANUARY

Code	Sales (Customer/Product)	Date	Amount

Notes:

Total Income $_____

FEBRUARY

Code	Sales (Customer/Product)	Date	Amount

Notes:

Total Income $_____

MARCH

Code	Sales (Customer/Product)	Date	Amount

Notes:

Total Income $_____

APRIL

Code	Sales (Customer/Product)	Date	Amount

Notes:

Total Income $_____

Code: F—Future Prospect/Project   L—Listing of a Sale   P—Pending Sale   S—Sold and Closed

MULTIPLE SALES MONTHLY PLANNER

MAY

Code	Sales (Customer/Product)	Date	Amount

Notes:

Total Income $_____

JUNE

Code	Sales (Customer/Product)	Date	Amount

Notes:

Total Income $_____

JULY

Code	Sales (Customer/Product)	Date	Amount

Notes:

Total Income $_____

AUGUST

Code	Sales (Customer/Product)	Date	Amount

Notes:

Total Income $_____

Code: F—Future Prospect/Project   L—Listing of a Sale   P—Pending Sale   S—Sold and Closed

MULTIPLE SALES MONTHLY PLANNER

SEPTEMBER

Code	Sales (Customer/Product)	Date	Amount

Notes:

Total Income $_____

OCTOBER

Code	Sales (Customer/Product)	Date	Amount

Notes:

Total Income $_____

NOVEMBER

Code	Sales (Customer/Product)	Date	Amount

Notes:

Total Income $_____

DECEMBER

Code	Sales (Customer/Product)	Date	Amount

Notes:

Total Income $_____

Code: F—Future Prospect/Project   L—Listing of a Sale   P—Pending Sale   S—Sold and Closed

Debt Payoff Record

*I*n two years' time we went from $16,000 debt to $2,000 (vehicles) and saved over $10,000. It took facing the numbers in the workbook, seeing what we spent every day, realizing how much money was going to finance charges, and getting out of our denial about debt. Now we still buy clothes and go on vacations. The difference is the planning and saving ahead of time.

WHEN TO USE THIS WORKSHEET

If you are beginning to get deep in debt or just need a better idea of how much you still owe on all your bills, such as medical expenses, car loan, finance company loan, credit cards, department store cards, etc., this worksheet is an important step for regaining financial control.

Staying organized is easier as well, as you now have a way to keep all your credit information in one simple place. You also can list the creditor's address and contact name, if you need this information frequently, in the blank space at the top or bottom of the page.

WHAT TO INCLUDE

The expenses to include are those you are unable to pay in full and must extend over a period of time (installment payments), such as automobile, home equity, student, or finance company loans; medical, legal, or family loans; IRS debt; and all credit card charges. This worksheet will clearly show you how much you have paid, what you still owe, and how much it is costing you to pay in installments. Remember, every penny you pay for finance charges is money you could have in your pocket for savings or vacations if the bills were paid in full.

HOW TO START

Start by filling in all the information at the top of the worksheet, such as the creditor's name and account number, for each debt you have. The "Total Balance Due" at the top gives you your starting figure so you can watch your progress. It will be helpful also to add the date somewhere on the top of this worksheet so you know your total beginning balance as of a specific date if you are not starting this form in January. Be sure to include the annual percentage rate (APR), which lets you know what interest rate you are paying.

As you make payments each month take time to actually look at your whole statement. I know the tendency is to zero in on the "Minimum Payment Due" block and ignore the rest. It's time to start paying attention to the other information on the statement like "New Balance," "Finance Charge," "Late Payment Fee," and "Over the Limit Fee." Granted, it's very difficult to acknowledge the whole picture, yet this is an important step and it's how you will begin to take charge and change your spending habits.

Fill in the "Amount Paid" and "Balance Due" for each month on this worksheet. The "Interest/Penalty" line is for all the finance charges and other fees. Just adding up that line across both pages will certainly get your attention each month.

Now really look at that statement and notice how much of the minimum payment you pay is for the finance charge and how much is actually payment toward the balance due. Amazing, isn't it? Now you see why it is taking so long to get out of debt.

COST OF CREDIT CARD PURCHASES

Have you ever wondered how long it would take to pay off your credit card debt? Chart A shows an example of what you would pay if you only paid the minimum payment on a $2,000 balance and then what you would pay with just an extra 25 cents a day, or about $7.50 a month.

When comparing the different minimum *percent* payments on Chart A, the smaller minimum percent (2%) certainly looks more appealing when looking at the resulting lower minimum payment ($40) for Card A. Now notice how much it adds to the "Total Interest Cost" ($7,636) and the number of "Years to Payoff" needed (42 years) to eliminate the debt. You can see why it really does take "forever" to pay off your debt!

The remainder of Chart A on the right shows the savings by just adding 25 cents a day to your minimum payment or $7.50 a month. For that same example mentioned above, you would save $4,916 in interest, not to mention the 28 years of payments that would be eliminated.

Now let's see what a difference even smaller amounts can make. If you added only 10 cents a day extra (that's only about $3 a month) to a $5,000 credit card balance, which had a 2 percent minimum payment

and a 17 percent interest rate, you would save $4,148 in interest!

Have I gotten your attention yet? The whole point is to increase those credit card payments above the minimum as much as you can. If you can pay the extra $100 or more each month, as many try to do, then go for it. If not, know that every effort you can make to pay some extra amount can have huge dividends for you in the long run.

Charts B and C are designed to show you it is possible to be debt free. In Chart B on page 61, an arbitrary 14 percent average is used for total debt, which could be a consolidation loan. My goal is to give you a sense of possibility. Find your total debt due in the left-hand column and then pick the amount you can afford each month, or the number of years you want to set as your goal to be debt free, in the columns to the right. Once you know that figure, you can start to do whatever it takes to make that monthly payment happen and get your debt paid off.

Let's say your goal is to be debt free in three or five years. Use Chart C on page 62 to find your interest rate and then pick your payments according to the three- or five-year plans.

There are many books on the market, software packages, and Web sites available to help you learn how to reduce your debt. These charts are provided merely as a sampling to motivate you to find the resources you need.

The information in these charts is from the authors of *Slash Your Debt: Save Money and Secure Your Future.*

CHART A: THE COST OF CREDIT CARD PURCHASES
BALANCE $2,000

			TOTAL COST WHEN PAYING ONLY THE MINIMUM PAYMENT			SAVINGS WHEN ADDING AN EXTRA $.25/DAY TO PAYMENT		
CARD	Interest Rate	Minimum Percent Payment	Minimum Payment	Total Interest Cost	YEARS* to Payoff	Interest Paid after Extra $.25/Day	Total Interest Saved	YEARS* Saved by Extra $.25/Day
CARD A	19.8%	2%	$40	$7,636	42	$2,720	$4,916	28
CARD B	19.8	2.78	56	2,585	17	1,557	1,029	8
CARD C	12.5	2	40	1,840	18	1,071	769	8
CARD D	8.25	3	60	542	10	400	142	3

*This information was in months, which was rounded up to make the extra year.

Source: *The Banker's Secret Credit Card Software.* This program makes it easy to crunch the numbers for your own credit cards, so you can see how much you can save by making payments greater than the required minimums. Available for PCs and Macs, $28 postpaid, 800-255-0899. <www.goodadvicepress.com>

CHART B: HOW SOON CAN YOU BE DEBT FREE?

The following figures are based on a debt with an average 14 percent interest rate.

If you want your debt paid off in the following years, see the chart below to find out how much your monthly payment would be to reach your debt-free goal.

Total Debt Due	1 Yr.	2 Yrs.	3 Yrs.	4 Yrs.	5 Yrs.	6 Yrs.	7 Yrs.	8 Yrs.	9 Yrs.	10 Yrs.
$ 3,000	$ 270	$ 144	$ 103	$ 82	$ 70	$ 62	$ 56	$ 52	$ 49	$ 47
5,000	449	240	171	137	116	103	94	87	82	78
10,000	898	480	342	273	233	206	187	174	163	155
15,000	1,347	720	513	410	349	309	281	261	245	233
20,000	1,796	960	684	547	465	412	375	347	327	311
25,000	2,245	1,200	854	683	582	515	469	434	408	388
30,000	2,694	1,440	1,025	820	698	618	562	521	490	466
35,000	3,143	1,680	1,196	956	814	721	656	608	572	543
40,000	3,591	1,921	1,367	1,093	931	824	750	695	653	621
45,000	4,040	2,161	1,538	1,230	1,047	927	843	782	735	699
50,000	4,489	2,401	1,709	1,366	1,163	1,030	937	869	817	776
75,000	6,734	3,601	2,563	2,049	1,745	1,545	1,406	1,303	1,225	1,165

Total Monthly Payment

Gerri Detweiler, Marc Eisenson, and Nancy Castleman have done a fantastic job of bringing together some of the most comprehensive, easy-to-read, and practical tips, examples, resources, and strategies I have seen. Using The Banker's Secret Credit Card Software for calculating, they provide nearly a dozen tables showing you how to reduce your credit card and mortgage debt.

GETTING OUT OF DEBT

After you pay off one debt, apply that same payment amount to another debt, preferably one with the highest interest, to shorten the term of that debt. An exception is if you have a smaller debt (even those with a lower interest rate) and you need the psychological satisfaction of making progress, then pay off that debt as soon as you can. As you continue to apply payments from paid-off debt to remaining debt, you will start to see how soon and how much of your total debt will be paid off in one or a few years.

By the following year, through the conscientious use of the worksheets in this workbook, you no longer may need this worksheet. Hurray! As one reader put it, "This Debt Payoff Record form makes the whole workbook worth hugging a thousand times!"

GETTING CONTROL OF YOUR FINANCES

When you reach the point where you become a wise and responsible consumer and you use credit to your advantage only as a means of using someone else's money and can pay the bill in full when it is due, you will know you truly have control of your finances! You also will have much greater peace of mind.

MAKING MONEY INSTEAD OF SPENDING MONEY

"Those who understand interest collect it, and those who don't pay it."

—William H. Stone

Once you have gotten into the habit of making payments and applying extra money from paid-off debt to reducing the remaining debt, you will have acquired

CHART C: PICK A MONTHLY PAYMENT TO PAY YOUR DEBT OFF IN THREE TO FIVE YEARS

Consolidation Loan Rate

Debt	Years	8%	9%	10%	11%	12%	13%	14%
$ 5,000	3	$ 157	$ 159	$ 161	$ 164	$ 166	$ 168	$ 171
	5	101	104	106	109	111	114	116
7,500	3	235	239	242	246	249	253	256
	5	152	156	159	163	167	171	175
10,000	3	313	318	323	327	332	337	342
	5	203	208	212	217	222	228	233
12,500	3	392	398	403	409	415	421	427
	5	253	259	266	272	278	284	291
15,000	3	470	477	484	491	498	505	513
	5	304	311	319	326	334	341	349
17,500	3	548	557	565	573	581	590	598
	5	355	363	372	381	389	398	407
20,000	3	627	636	645	655	664	674	684
	5	406	415	425	435	445	455	465
25,000	3	783	795	807	818	830	842	854
	5	507	519	531	544	556	569	582
30,000	3	940	954	968	982	996	1,011	1,025
	5	608	623	637	652	667	683	698
35,000	3	1,097	1,113	1,129	1,146	1,163	1,179	1,196
	5	710	727	744	761	779	796	814
40,000	3	1,253	1,272	1,291	1,310	1,329	1,348	1,367
	5	811	830	850	870	890	910	931
45,000	3	1,410	1,431	1,452	1,473	1,495	1,516	1,538
	5	912	934	956	978	1,001	1,024	1,047
50,000	3	1,567	1,590	1,613	1,637	1,661	1,685	1,709
	5	1,014	1,038	1,062	1,087	1,112	1,138	1,163

Source: This table is reprinted with permission from *Slash Your Debt: Save Money & Secure Your Future* (1999, Financial Literacy Center, $10.95 <www.slashyourdebt.com>).

a great skill. When your debts are paid off, you can continue the payment schedule, only this time putting money into your savings and investments. All that money that was used to pay off the debt-plus-interest and penalty charges now can go toward your savings for you. Instead of spending money, you actually will be making money on the same payment amounts.

Let's see what kind of money you could be making. Chart D gives you an idea of just how much money. Using the same $2,000 credit card balance example from Chart A, look what can happen if you *invested* $2,000 at 10 percent instead of *spending* $2,000 at 19.8 percent. Rather than paying off the $2,000 debt for 42 years and *paying* $7,636 in interest, you would be *earning* $131,072 (compounded monthly) in 40 years. Not bad for only a $2,000 investment.

CHART D
$2,000 One-Time Investment—
No Annual Contributions

Years	6%	10%	14%
10	$ 3,639	$ 5,414	$ 8,045
20	6,620	14,656	32,361
30	12,045	39,675	130,169
40	24,702	131,072	691,672

Calculations were compounded monthly.

Source: These figures were calculated by Marc Eisenson of <www.goodadvicepress.com>, author of *The Banker's Secret*, and coauthor of *Slash Your Debt: Save Money & Secure Your Future*, and *Invest in Yourself: Six Secrets to a Rich Life*.

The same goes for comparing earnings in Chart D with the example of paying off debt with a 14 percent interest rate in Chart B. By researching and finding higher investment returns, you can see the payoff for investing over 10 to 40 years.

Best of all, not only will you have assets instead of debts, you will feel encouraged, excited, and confident about your financial skills.

Thank you for getting us jump-started! It was most helpful to see which debts to focus on so we could prioritize our debt-payoff plan. We buckled down to really change and pay attention to our spending, and now we are so inspired to pay off our final debts that we have hired a financial planner to help us invest our new-found money.

GETTING ONLINE HELP

As of this printing, the following Internet-based nonprofit organizations provide financial information, services, counseling (including by phone), and support. Their programs are designed to help you make one payment, reduce the amount of the monthly creditor payments, and get debt paid off early. Fees range from free to nominal.

My Vesta (formerly Debt Counselors of America)
<www.myvesta.org>   800-680-3328
My Vesta offers far more than debt counseling with their One-Pay®, Crisis Relief Team℠, Financial Recovery Counseling, Online Bill Management, The Ultimate Spending Plan, and the Debt Eliminator® Report services.

National Foundation for Credit Counseling (NFCC)
<www.nfcc.org>   800-388-2227
NFCC is the nation's oldest and largest nonprofit credit counseling organization and is the umbrella for the numerous Consumer Credit Counseling Service (CCCS) agencies throughout the nation. You can make an in-office appointment in your area or receive online counseling. One of their many services includes the Debt Solver Program™. Their Web site links you to other resourceful sites.

Genus
<www.genus.org>   800-210-4455
Genus offers their Debt Management Program along with many other educational and mortgage services. The Web site offers some handy and practical calculators for credit card payoff, loan payoff, and creating budgets.

DEBT PAYOFF RECORD

	Loans			Credit Cards		
CREDITOR						
Account Number						
Total Balance Due						
Phone Number						
Interest Rate (APR)						
January						
Amount Paid						
Interest/Penalty						
Balance Due						
February						
Amount Paid						
Interest/Penalty						
Balance Due						
March						
Amount Paid						
Interest/Penalty						
Balance Due						
April						
Amount Paid						
Interest/Penalty						
Balance Due						
May						
Amount Paid						
Interest/Penalty						
Balance Due						
June						
Amount Paid						
Interest/Penalty						
Balance Due						
July						
Amount Paid						
Interest/Penalty						
Balance Due						
August						
Amount Paid						
Interest/Penalty						
Balance Due						
September						
Amount Paid						
Interest/Penalty						
Balance Due						
October						
Amount Paid						
Interest/Penalty						
Balance Due						
November						
Amount Paid						
Interest/Penalty						
Balance Due						
December						
Amount Paid						
Interest/Penalty						
Balance Due						
Balance Due						

DEBT PAYOFF RECORD

Other (Medical, Legal, Personal, etc.)

						Total

Debt Repayment Worksheet

Once you have completed the top part of the Debt Payoff Record on the previous pages and outlined all of your debt, it may be overwhelming to stop and see the total amount of debt to be paid off. If you are in a situation where there is not enough disposable money each month to even pay the monthly minimums, and you are determined to pay back your debt in full, know that there *is* a solution.

The Debt Repayment Worksheet is provided to help when you are in a very tight financial situation and choose not to declare bankruptcy or use the services of any nonprofit credit counseling agency. This approach will take time and patience. The payoff, however, will be preservation of your personal and financial integrity.

This repayment concept has been discussed and outlined very well and over time in Jerrold Mundis's *How to Get Out of Debt, Stay Out of Debt and Live Prosperously* and Dave Ramsey's *The Financial PeacePlanner* books. The Debt Repayment Worksheet summarizes how to work out a fair share repayment plan for all of your creditors using what disposable money you have available to pay off your debt.

HOW TO USE THIS WORKSHEET

First, fill out your Monthly Budget Worksheet (starting on page 36), so you know exactly how much your monthly bills and expenses are. Next, determine how much money you can use to pay toward your debt. With this figure and your total balances from the Debt Payoff Record beginning on page 64, we will work out each creditor's percentage and the amount of money you have available for paying them.

To make this method work, there are four things you need to do:

1. Contact each creditor and explain your plan by including a copy of your budget, the first payment check, and this outline of debt repayment.

2. Stay honest and stick to your commitment religiously, and make every one of these monthly payments on time.

3. Track and manage your spending very diligently.

4. Do not incur any new debt.

It also doesn't hurt to pray in your own way!

During this repayment period it also will be important to find ways to raise some extra cash to pay toward your debt or to cover the surprise incidentals that come up, whether through selling items, holding yard sales, working overtime, or getting part-time work, and to apply any extra money from gifts, rebates, or refunds toward this debt as well. In the future you will have the opportunity again to treat yourself with that gift money. For now you are trading a piece of furniture or jewelry for some peace of mind.

If your creditors resist the nominal payment amounts (for example, they are asking for payments of $100 and you are sending $35), persist with your program and keep making payments. Hold the goal of being debt free and keep knowing that you can pay off your debt slowly and methodically. Continue to explain and show your plan and follow through with it.

You can't be forced to pay money you do not have. Once you start paying more to a particularly aggressive creditor, the whole repayment plan will go out of balance and you will be back in the familiar discouraging debt cycle again.

Keep in mind this financial condition will eventually pass. Amazingly, you will find that these initial small amounts of payments start to increase as you slowly begin to pay off debt and work with a program. As each creditor gets paid in full over time, keep adjusting and increasing your payments accordingly and you will start to see those balances go down. Stop and realize that you are now getting *out of debt* instead of into debt, and notice how you are starting to regain a solid sense of control in your life once again.

As Winston Churchill once said: "Never, never, never give up!"

DEBT REPAYMENT WORKSHEET

Step 1   Disposable Income
Total Amount of Disposable Income Available to Pay Off Debt: $_____
(Calculate your budget on the Monthly Budget Worksheet beginning on page 36.)

Step 2   Total Combined Debt
Total Amount of All Debt Combined: $_____
(Transfer the total from the Debt Payoff Record beginning on page 64.)

Step 3   New Payment
List below the total balances you owe each creditor starting with the smallest balance and then follow the formula to determine the new payment for each creditor.

Creditor	Balance Due	÷ Total Combined Debt	= Share Percent (of Total Combined Debt)	× Disposable Income	New Payment
Dentist	$500	÷ $11,500	= 4.3%	× $700	= $30.43
Visa	$1,500	÷ 11,500	= 13%	× $700	= $91.30

Credit Card Purchase Record

To avoid a shocking bill at the end of the month, keep careful track of your credit card charges. This way, you can anticipate what the bill will be and prepare for it by making the appropriate adjustments in your spending and your planning.

CREDIT CARD PURCHASE RECORD

JAN.		FEB.		MAR.		APR.		MAY		JUNE	
Billing Cycle Closing Date: ① _____		_____		_____		_____		_____		_____	
Purchase	Amount	Purchase	Amount	Purchase	Amount	Purchase	Amount	Purchase	Amount	Purchase	Amount
③ 3/gas ②	14.91										
7/Shoes	20.82										
Total											

By knowing the status of your charges at all times, you become much more selective and careful about impulse charging. When you reach this point, you know that you have learned how to keep from getting overextended and have taken one more step toward controlling your finances.

HOW TO USE THIS CHART

① First find out and enter the "Billing Cycle Closing
② Date." Then record all charges made during the month until that date so you know which purchases will be included on that month's upcoming bill. Purchases charged after that closing date should be entered in the next month's column (the month for which you actually will be billed). Jot down in the corner the date ③ you made the charge.

Remember, this chart is flexible. If you use different cards frequently, then divide the monthly column into the necessary parts to keep the separate records, or use the duplicate chart that follows for your multiple credit card use. You also can carry an extra check register with you to record your charges for other cards. Make the chart work for you!

CREDIT CARD PURCHASE RECORD

JULY		AUG.		SEPT.		OCT.		NOV.		DEC.	
Purchase	Amount	Purchase	Amount	Purchase	Amount	Purchase	Amount	Purchase	Amount	Purchase	Amount
Total											

CREDIT CARD PURCHASE RECORD

JAN.		FEB.		MAR.		APR.		MAY		JUNE	
Billing Cycle Closing Date: ___		___		___		___		___		___	
Purchase	Amount	Purchase	Amount	Purchase	Amount	Purchase	Amount	Purchase	Amount	Purchase	Amount
Total											

CREDIT CARD PURCHASE RECORD

JULY		AUG.		SEPT.		OCT.		NOV.		DEC.	
Billing Cycle Closing Date:											
Purchase	Amount	Purchase	Amount	Purchase	Amount	Purchase	Amount	Purchase	Amount	Purchase	Amount
Total											

Monthly Expense Record

Sometimes it takes the black-and-white approach to get someone's attention. Connie started using the workbook to track expenses and plan ahead when she and her husband knew they would be retiring in a few years. Her husband was staggered when he saw the expenses they both spent for six months. He was finally ready to sit down and outline and plan the finances together with Connie. They also successfully started saving for their travel plans. The workbook became an effective communication tool—a way for getting out of the dream world and back into reality.

FINDING OUT WHERE ALL THE MONEY GOES

How many times have you asked yourself "Where did all the money go?" Even keeping detailed records in the check register doesn't always give a clear answer to that question. With these worksheets and with some firm self-discipline, you will easily and very graphically know exactly where all your money has gone as well as how much money has come in.

Begin by picking a time every day to jot down all the spending for that day. Some people like to carry a small notebook to record all their daily cash. Others use my book *Money Tracker: A Quick and Easy Way to Keep Tabs on Your Spending* to record cash for the week and then transfer the totals to this worksheet. With practice and determination, you will develop the habit of regularly recording all *cash, debits, checks,* and *charged* expenses. At first this may seem time-consuming and uncomfortable. However, once you get past the 21-

day marker for creating a new habit, you will notice that your recording literally takes only minutes a day.

Be patient with yourself and the results. The first month or two your numbers may not be perfect, but the habit is being developed and information is emerging. By the third month you will be amazed at the results.

There is something about the act of manually recording your expenses each day (versus waiting until the end of the week or month and trying to record a pocketful of receipts) that makes a significant difference. As you physically write down the numbers, you are actually taking in a lot of information with your different senses. Visually you see all the other entries in the column and subconsciously start to note all the money already spent to date. This alone is enough to change your attitude and spending habits and help slow down the spending.

Your payoff will be the sense of control you have over your finances and finally being aware of your overall spending. Many people insist that once they began tracking their spending, they started spending less and saving more.

Recording cash spent is important. Every time you write a check for cash or use the automated teller machine (ATM), write down where you actually spend that cash. Itemizing all the cash provides more valuable information for you than just recording "$50 cash" or "misc." six times as an expense and not really knowing how it was spent or "where the money went."

Debit cards and ATMs as conveniences can be either a blessing or a curse depending how you use them. After months of total chaos and overdraft charges in the checking account, one couple worked out their monthly budget to determine exactly how much cash was needed each week. On Mondays Joe gets his lump cash and knows it has to cover his gas, coffee, meals, snacks, and all other incidentals for the week. Ginny sticks with the checkbook. Both are relieved to finally always know their current balance in the checkbook.

If you seem to have more month than money most of the time, remember your choices. You can reduce, postpone, modify, or eliminate your spending. If you are not sure where to begin, a review of these filled-out worksheets will quickly show you which optional categories to start with. Maybe you need to do more of your own home or car repairs, be more energy-conscious, eat out less, cut back on gifts, start carpooling, or do whatever fits your abilities and interests. When you do cut back, the results will be noticed immediately.

As you work with these worksheets, modify them to fit your unique lifestyles. The expense categories, net income, savings, investment, and retirement sections are all provided as guidelines to set up your own system.

If you have tax-deductible expenses, note them here. If you want all you tax records kept together, you can use the handy **Tax-Deductible Expense Record** in Part Three.

You will notice the emphasis on net income, not on gross income, throughout this workbook. The idea is to deal only with actual money and not record more information than you need to. The gross income in-

formation is usually on your check stubs. If you need to keep a record of your taxes, FICA, retirement savings, and other deductions, you can use the "End-of-the-Year Tax Information" section on the bottom of the **Summary-for-the-Year Record** worksheet following these monthly expense pages.

I like using a color code like a highlighter or some key symbols to designate where the money came from to pay for certain expenses. It helps me know when I used money from our reserve account or household savings account. That way I feel I'm working with a plan and can see how the extra expenses are planned and covered.

How Do I Compare to Others?

My readers and clients have often wanted to compare their spending to others. These studies and figures do exist from various agencies. The most convenient source I have seen is a chart called "How Americans Spend and Save," which includes almost all incomes and categories. This chart is in the book *It's Never Too . . . Late to Wake Up and Smell the Money: Fresh Starts at Any Age—and Any Season of Your Life* by Ginger Applegarth with Leslie Whitaker (published by Penguin USA 2000).

MONTHLY EXPENSE RECORD

Balance Forward from Last Month:
Cash $37.00   Checking $62.00   Savings $11,796.45

NET INCOME

SALARY/COMMISSIONS	Chris	Kim	TOTAL
	896.00		
		1,407.43	
	883.00		
		1,407.43	
TOTAL INCOME			4,593.86

OTHER			
Yard Sale—273			273.00
TOTAL INCOME			4,866.86

SAVINGS

(Describe)	
Reserve (used other $257 this month)	750.00
Goals	75.00
Emergency	215.00
TOTAL SAVINGS	1,040.00

INVESTMENTS/RETIREMENT

(See Payroll Deduction)	
TOTAL INVESTMENTS	

FOOD / HOUSEHOLD / TRANSPORTATION / PERSONAL / MEDICAL

		groceries	meals out, school lunches	tobacco alcohol snacks beverages	mainten. house yard pool	appliances furniture furnishings supplies	misc. postage copies bank chg. film	interest taxes	gas	auto mainten. wash license	transit tolls parking	clothing alterations dry clean. laundry shoe care	toiletries cosmetics hair nails massage	doctor dentist medicine vitamins	personal growth therapy
WEEK 1	1	40.00	15.00						13.92						
	2		7.50		20.34	33.67									
	3	5.94							9.35				25.00		65.30
	4			15.31						24.73		21.82		10.20	
	5		28.98												
	6			5.10											
	7	44.48		6.05								15.03			
WEEK 2	8													33.68	
	9	67.10	7.50				29.00					43.98			
	10								14.79						
	11	7.25	14.22										19.00		
	12			4.95										13.00	
	13			5.10	14.76					6.95					
	14			6.05											
WEEK 3	15	10.53											21.46		
	16		12.35						10.45			20.80			
	17														
	18	28.55	7.50	5.10											
	19												25.00		
	20	9.57										13.57			
	21					23.00									65.30
WEEK 4	22			11.08					15.65						
	23				10.45										
	24														
	25	149.73													
	26		7.50	4.95					9.35			15.41			
	27						8.50								
	28	19.52													
	29				4.31										
	30	67.10	27.34						19.95						
	31	8.59													
Total		458.36	127.89	63.69	49.86	56.67	37.50	—	93.46	31.68	—	130.41	90.46	56.88	130.60

MONTHLY EXPENSE RECORD

FIXED EXPENSES

Monthly	Amount	Monthly	Amount
Mortgage/Rent	784.00	Insurance:	
Assn. Fee		House/Apt	
Gas/Fuel	73.00	Auto	
Electricity	89.00	Life	54.00
Water/Refuse		Health (Payroll ded.)	
Garbage/Sewer		Dental	
Telephone	53.21	Disability	
Cellular Phone			
Cable/Satellite	35.00	Storage	75
Internet			
Child Support			
Spousal Support			
TOTAL	1,034.21	**TOTAL**	129.00

INSTALLMENT EXPENSES

Loans/Credit Cards	Amount
Visa	75.00
MC	50.00
Student Loan	167.00
Car Payment	291.00
TOTAL	583.00

TOTAL EXPENSES

Total Fixed Expenses	1,163.21
Total Installment Expenses	583.00
Total Monthly Expenses from Below	1,932.05
GRAND TOTAL	3,678.26

+ Savings (1040.00) = $4,718.26

	RECREATION		EDUCATION				CHILDREN			GENERAL			
vacation trips	entertain. video movie tapes CDs	lottery sports hobbies lessons clubs	computer upgrades software supplies service	seminar workshop tuition supplies	books magazines software	child care sitter	tutor allowance toys school expense	pet vet supplies	gifts cards flowers	charitable contribut. church	work expense dues	prof. services legal CPA investment	other (expla-nation)
1							10.00			50.00			
2	3.21								40.00				
3													
4													
5							10.00						
6													
7										50.00			
8							3.57						
9		19.22											
10									3.59				
11					15.22								
12							10.00						
13										50.00			
14									10.56				
15							15.98						
16													
17	15.04												
18					23.78		10.00						
19									2.60	50.00			
20													
21													
22					39.00								
23							4.98						
24													
25										40.00			
26													
27							10.00						
28	57.84												
29													
30													
31										60.00			
Total	—	76.09	19.22	—	—	78.00	—	74.53	—	56.75	300.00	—	—	—

MONTHLY EXPENSE RECORD

Balance Forward from Last Month:
Cash _____ Checking _____ Savings _____

NET INCOME

			TOTAL
SALARY/COMMISSIONS			
		TOTAL INCOME	
OTHER			
		TOTAL INCOME	

SAVINGS

(Describe)	
TOTAL SAVINGS	

INVESTMENTS/RETIREMENT

TOTAL INVESTMENTS	

FOOD   HOUSEHOLD   TRANSPORTATION   PERSONAL   MEDICAL

	groceries	meals out, school lunches	tobacco alcohol snacks beverages	mainten. house yard pool	appliances furniture furnishings supplies	misc. postage copies bank chg. film	interest taxes	gas	auto mainten. wash license	transit tolls parking	clothing alterations dry clean. laundry shoe care	toiletries cosmetics hair nails massage	doctor dentist medicine vitamins	personal growth therapy
WEEK 1 — 1														
2														
3														
4														
5														
6														
7														
WEEK 2 — 8														
9														
10														
11														
12														
13														
14														
WEEK 3 — 15														
16														
17														
18														
19														
20														
21														
WEEK 4 — 22														
23														
24														
25														
26														
27														
28														
29														
30														
31														
Total														

MONTHLY EXPENSE RECORD

FIXED EXPENSES

Monthly	Amount	Monthly	Amount
Mortgage/Rent		Insurance:	
Assn. Fee		House/Apt	
Gas/Fuel		Auto	
Electricity		Life	
Water/Refuse		Health	
Garbage/Sewer		Dental	
Telephone		Disability	
Cellular Phone			
Cable/Satellite			
Internet			
Child Support			
Spousal Support			
TOTAL		**TOTAL**	

INSTALLMENT EXPENSES

Loans/Credit Cards	Amount
TOTAL	

TOTAL EXPENSES

Total Fixed Expenses	
Total Installment Expenses	
Total Monthly Expenses from Below	
GRAND TOTAL	

RECREATION   EDUCATION   CHILDREN   GENERAL

	vacation trips	entertain. video movie tapes CDs	lottery sports hobbies lessons clubs	computer upgrades software supplies service	seminar workshop tuition supplies	books magazines software	child care sitter	tutor allowance toys school expense	pet vet supplies	gifts cards flowers	charitable contribut. church	work expense dues	prof. services legal CPA investment	other (expla-nation)
1														
2														
3														
4														
5														
6														
7														
8														
9														
10														
11														
12														
13														
14														
15														
16														
17														
18														
19														
20														
21														
22														
23														
24														
25														
26														
27														
28														
29														
30														
31														
Total														

MONTHLY EXPENSE RECORD

Balance Forward from Last Month:
Cash _____ Checking _____ Savings _____

NET INCOME

			TOTAL
SALARY/COMMISSIONS			
		TOTAL INCOME	
OTHER			
		TOTAL INCOME	

SAVINGS

(Describe)	
TOTAL SAVINGS	

INVESTMENTS/RETIREMENT

TOTAL INVESTMENTS	

FOOD · HOUSEHOLD · TRANSPORTATION · PERSONAL · MEDICAL

	groceries	meals out, school lunches	tobacco alcohol snacks beverages	mainten. house yard pool	appliances furniture furnishings supplies	misc. postage copies bank chg. film	interest taxes	gas	auto mainten. wash license	transit tolls parking	clothing alterations dry clean. laundry shoe care	toiletries cosmetics hair nails massage	doctor dentist medicine vitamins	personal growth therapy	
1															
2															
3															
4															
5															
6															
7															
8															
9															
10															
11															
12															
13															
14															
15															
16															
17															
18															
19															
20															
21															
22															
23															
24															
25															
26															
27															
28															
29															
30															
31															
Total															

WEEK 1, WEEK 2, WEEK 3, WEEK 4

MONTHLY EXPENSE RECORD

FIXED EXPENSES

Monthly	Amount	Monthly	Amount
Mortgage/Rent		Insurance:	
Assn. Fee		House/Apt	
Gas/Fuel		Auto	
Electricity		Life	
Water/Refuse		Health	
Garbage/Sewer		Dental	
Telephone		Disability	
Cellular Phone			
Cable/Satellite			
Internet			
Child Support			
Spousal Support			
TOTAL		**TOTAL**	

INSTALLMENT EXPENSES

Loans/Credit Cards	Amount
TOTAL	

TOTAL EXPENSES

Total Fixed Expenses	
Total Installment Expenses	
Total Monthly Expenses from Below	
GRAND TOTAL	

RECREATION — EDUCATION — CHILDREN — GENERAL

	vacation trips	entertain. video movie tapes CDs	lottery sports hobbies lessons clubs	computer upgrades software supplies service	seminar workshop tuition supplies	books magazines software	child care sitter	tutor allowance toys school expense	pet vet supplies	gifts cards flowers	charitable contribut. church	work expense dues	prof. services legal CPA investment	other (expla-nation)
1														
2														
3														
4														
5														
6														
7														
8														
9														
10														
11														
12														
13														
14														
15														
16														
17														
18														
19														
20														
21														
22														
23														
24														
25														
26														
27														
28														
29														
30														
31														
Total														

MONTHLY EXPENSE RECORD

Balance Forward from Last Month:
Cash _____ Checking _____ Savings _____

NET INCOME

			TOTAL
SALARY/COMMISSIONS			
TOTAL INCOME			
OTHER			
TOTAL INCOME			

SAVINGS

(Describe)	
TOTAL SAVINGS	

INVESTMENTS/RETIREMENT

TOTAL INVESTMENTS	

FOOD · HOUSEHOLD · TRANSPORTATION · PERSONAL · MEDICAL

	groceries	meals out, school lunches	tobacco alcohol snacks beverages	mainten. house yard pool	appliances furniture furnishings supplies	misc. postage copies bank chg. film	interest taxes	gas	auto mainten. wash license	transit tolls parking	clothing alterations dry clean. laundry shoe care	toiletries cosmetics hair nails massage	doctor dentist medicine vitamins	personal growth therapy
W 1														
E 2														
E 3														
K 4														
5														
1 6														
7														
W 8														
E 9														
E 10														
K 11														
12														
2 13														
14														
W 15														
E 16														
E 17														
K 18														
19														
3 20														
21														
W 22														
E 23														
E 24														
K 25														
26														
4 27														
28														
29														
30														
31														
Total														

MONTHLY EXPENSE RECORD

FIXED EXPENSES

Monthly	Amount	Monthly	Amount
Mortgage/Rent		Insurance:	
Assn. Fee		House/Apt	
Gas/Fuel		Auto	
Electricity		Life	
Water/Refuse		Health	
Garbage/Sewer		Dental	
Telephone		Disability	
Cellular Phone			
Cable/Satellite			
Internet			
Child Support			
Spousal Support			
TOTAL		**TOTAL**	

INSTALLMENT EXPENSES

Loans/Credit Cards	Amount
TOTAL	

TOTAL EXPENSES

Total Fixed Expenses	
Total Installment Expenses	
Total Monthly Expenses from Below	
GRAND TOTAL	

RECREATION   EDUCATION   CHILDREN   GENERAL

	vacation trips	entertain. video movie tapes CDs	lottery sports hobbies lessons clubs	computer upgrades software supplies service	seminar workshop tuition supplies	books magazines software	child care sitter	tutor allowance toys school expense	pet vet supplies	gifts cards flowers	charitable contribut. church	work expense dues	prof. services legal CPA investment	other (expla- nation)
1														
2														
3														
4														
5														
6														
7														
8														
9														
10														
11														
12														
13														
14														
15														
16														
17														
18														
19														
20														
21														
22														
23														
24														
25														
26														
27														
28														
29														
30														
31														
Total														

MONTHLY EXPENSE RECORD   81

MONTHLY EXPENSE RECORD

Balance Forward from Last Month:
Cash _____ Checking _____ Savings _____

NET INCOME

			TOTAL
SALARY/COMMISSIONS			
·			
TOTAL INCOME			
OTHER			
TOTAL INCOME			

SAVINGS

(Describe)	
TOTAL SAVINGS	

INVESTMENTS/RETIREMENT

TOTAL INVESTMENTS	

FOOD · HOUSEHOLD · TRANSPORTATION · PERSONAL · MEDICAL

	groceries	meals out, school lunches	tobacco alcohol snacks beverages	mainten. house yard pool	appliances furniture furnishings supplies	misc. postage copies bank chg. film	interest taxes	gas	auto mainten. wash license	transit tolls parking	clothing alterations dry clean. laundry shoe care	toiletries cosmetics hair nails massage	doctor dentist medicine vitamins	personal growth therapy
W 1														
E 2														
E 3														
K 4														
5														
1 6														
7														
W 8														
E 9														
E 10														
K 11														
12														
2 13														
14														
W 15														
E 16														
E 17														
K 18														
19														
3 20														
21														
W 22														
E 23														
E 24														
K 25														
26														
4 27														
28														
29														
30														
31														
Total														

MONTHLY EXPENSE RECORD

FIXED EXPENSES

Monthly	Amount	Monthly	Amount
Mortgage/Rent		Insurance:	
Assn. Fee		House/Apt	
Gas/Fuel		Auto	
Electricity		Life	
Water/Refuse		Health	
Garbage/Sewer		Dental	
Telephone		Disability	
Cellular Phone			
Cable/Satellite			
Internet			
Child Support			
Spousal Support			
TOTAL		**TOTAL**	

INSTALLMENT EXPENSES

Loans/Credit Cards	Amount
TOTAL	

TOTAL EXPENSES

Total Fixed Expenses	
Total Installment Expenses	
Total Monthly Expenses from Below	
GRAND TOTAL	

RECREATION   EDUCATION   CHILDREN   GENERAL

	vacation trips	entertain. video movie tapes CDs	lottery sports hobbies lessons clubs	computer upgrades software supplies service	seminar workshop tuition supplies	books magazines software	child care sitter	tutor allowance toys school expense	pet vet supplies	gifts cards flowers	charitable contribut. church	work expense dues	prof. services legal CPA investment	other (expla-nation)
1														
2														
3														
4														
5														
6														
7														
8														
9														
10														
11														
12														
13														
14														
15														
16														
17														
18														
19														
20														
21														
22														
23														
24														
25														
26														
27														
28														
29														
30														
31														
Total														

MONTHLY EXPENSE RECORD

Balance Forward from Last Month:
Cash _____ Checking _____ Savings _____

NET INCOME

			TOTAL
SALARY/COMMISSIONS			
TOTAL INCOME			
OTHER			
TOTAL INCOME			

SAVINGS

(Describe)	
TOTAL SAVINGS	

INVESTMENTS/RETIREMENT

TOTAL INVESTMENTS	

FOOD | HOUSEHOLD | TRANSPORTATION | PERSONAL | MEDICAL

	groceries	meals out, school lunches	tobacco alcohol snacks beverages	mainten. house yard pool	appliances furniture furnishings supplies	misc. postage copies bank chg. film	interest taxes	gas	auto mainten. wash license	transit tolls parking	clothing alterations dry clean. laundry shoe care	toiletries cosmetics hair nails massage	doctor dentist medicine vitamins	personal growth therapy
WEEK 1 1														
2														
3														
4														
5														
6														
7														
WEEK 2 8														
9														
10														
11														
12														
13														
14														
WEEK 3 15														
16														
17														
18														
19														
20														
21														
WEEK 4 22														
23														
24														
25														
26														
27														
28														
29														
30														
31														
Total														

MONTHLY EXPENSE RECORD

FIXED EXPENSES

Monthly	Amount	Monthly	Amount
Mortgage/Rent		Insurance:	
Assn. Fee		House/Apt	
Gas/Fuel		Auto	
Electricity		Life	
Water/Refuse		Health	
Garbage/Sewer		Dental	
Telephone		Disability	
Cellular Phone			
Cable/Satellite			
Internet			
Child Support			
Spousal Support			
TOTAL		**TOTAL**	

INSTALLMENT EXPENSES

Loans/Credit Cards	Amount
TOTAL	

TOTAL EXPENSES

Total Fixed Expenses	
Total Installment Expenses	
Total Monthly Expenses from Below	
GRAND TOTAL	

RECREATION · EDUCATION · CHILDREN · GENERAL

	vacation trips	entertain. video movie tapes CDs	lottery sports hobbies lessons clubs	computer upgrades software supplies service	seminar workshop tuition supplies	books magazines software	child care sitter	tutor allowance toys school expense	pet vet supplies	gifts cards flowers	charitable contribut. church	work expense dues	prof. services legal CPA investment	other (expla-nation)
1														
2														
3														
4														
5														
6														
7														
8														
9														
10														
11														
12														
13														
14														
15														
16														
17														
18														
19														
20														
21														
22														
23														
24														
25														
26														
27														
28														
29														
30														
31														
Total														

MONTHLY EXPENSE RECORD

Balance Forward from Last Month:
Cash _____ Checking _____ Savings _____

NET INCOME

			TOTAL
SALARY/COMMISSIONS			
		TOTAL INCOME	
OTHER			
		TOTAL INCOME	

SAVINGS

(Describe)	
TOTAL SAVINGS	

INVESTMENTS/RETIREMENT

TOTAL INVESTMENTS	

FOOD | HOUSEHOLD | TRANSPORTATION | PERSONAL | MEDICAL

	groceries	meals out, school lunches	tobacco alcohol snacks beverages	mainten. house yard pool	appliances furniture furnishings supplies	misc. postage copies bank chg. film	interest taxes	gas	auto mainten. wash license	transit tolls parking	clothing alterations dry clean. laundry shoe care	toiletries cosmetics hair nails massage	doctor dentist medicine vitamins	personal growth therapy
W 1														
E 2														
E 3														
K 4														
5														
1 6														
7														
W 8														
E 9														
E 10														
K 11														
12														
2 13														
14														
W 15														
E 16														
E 17														
K 18														
19														
3 20														
21														
W 22														
E 23														
E 24														
K 25														
26														
4 27														
28														
29														
30														
31														
Total														

MONTHLY EXPENSE RECORD

FIXED EXPENSES

Monthly	Amount	Monthly	Amount
Mortgage/Rent		Insurance:	
Assn. Fee		House/Apt	
Gas/Fuel		Auto	
Electricity		Life	
Water/Refuse		Health	
Garbage/Sewer		Dental	
Telephone		Disability	
Cellular Phone			
Cable/Satellite			
Internet			
Child Support			
Spousal Support			
TOTAL		**TOTAL**	

INSTALLMENT EXPENSES

Loans/Credit Cards	Amount
TOTAL	

TOTAL EXPENSES

Total Fixed Expenses	
Total Installment Expenses	
Total Monthly Expenses from Below	
GRAND TOTAL	

RECREATION   EDUCATION   CHILDREN   GENERAL

	vacation trips	entertain. video movie tapes CDs	lottery sports hobbies lessons clubs	computer upgrades software supplies service	seminar workshop tuition supplies	books magazines software	child care sitter	tutor allowance toys school expense	pet vet supplies	gifts cards flowers	charitable contribut. church	work expense dues	prof. services legal CPA investment	other (expla-nation)
1														
2														
3														
4														
5														
6														
7														
8														
9														
10														
11														
12														
13														
14														
15														
16														
17														
18														
19														
20														
21														
22														
23														
24														
25														
26														
27														
28														
29														
30														
31														
Total														

MONTHLY EXPENSE RECORD

Balance Forward from Last Month:
Cash _____ Checking _____ Savings _____

NET INCOME

			TOTAL
SALARY/COMMISSIONS			
	TOTAL INCOME		
OTHER			
	TOTAL INCOME		

SAVINGS

(Describe)	
TOTAL SAVINGS	

INVESTMENTS/RETIREMENT

TOTAL INVESTMENTS	

FOOD			HOUSEHOLD					TRANSPORTATION			PERSONAL		MEDICAL	
groceries	meals out, school lunches	tobacco alcohol snacks beverages	mainten. house yard pool	appliances furniture furnishings supplies	misc. postage copies bank chg. film	interest taxes	gas	auto mainten. wash license	transit tolls parking	clothing alterations dry clean. laundry shoe care	toiletries cosmetics hair nails massage	doctor dentist medicine vitamins	personal growth therapy

WEEK 1														
1														
2														
3														
4														
5														
6														
7														
WEEK 2														
8														
9														
10														
11														
12														
13														
14														
WEEK 3														
15														
16														
17														
18														
19														
20														
21														
WEEK 4														
22														
23														
24														
25														
26														
27														
28														
29														
30														
31														
Total														

MONTHLY EXPENSE RECORD

FIXED EXPENSES

Monthly	Amount	Monthly	Amount
Mortgage/Rent		Insurance:	
Assn. Fee		House/Apt	
Gas/Fuel		Auto	
Electricity		Life	
Water/Refuse		Health	
Garbage/Sewer		Dental	
Telephone		Disability	
Cellular Phone			
Cable/Satellite			
Internet			
Child Support			
Spousal Support			
TOTAL		**TOTAL**	

INSTALLMENT EXPENSES

Loans/Credit Cards	Amount
TOTAL	

TOTAL EXPENSES

Total Fixed Expenses	
Total Installment Expenses	
Total Monthly Expenses from Below	
GRAND TOTAL	

RECREATION   EDUCATION   CHILDREN   GENERAL

	vacation trips	entertain. video movie tapes CDs	lottery sports hobbies lessons clubs	computer upgrades software supplies service	seminar workshop tuition supplies	books magazines software	child care sitter	tutor allowance toys school expense	pet vet supplies	gifts cards flowers	charitable contribut. church	work expense dues	prof. services legal CPA investment	other (expla-nation)
1														
2														
3														
4														
5														
6														
7														
8														
9														
10														
11														
12														
13														
14														
15														
16														
17														
18														
19														
20														
21														
22														
23														
24														
25														
26														
27														
28														
29														
30														
31														
Total														

MONTHLY EXPENSE RECORD

Balance Forward from Last Month:
Cash _____ Checking _____ Savings _____

NET INCOME

				TOTAL
SALARY/COMMISSIONS				
		TOTAL INCOME		
OTHER				
		TOTAL INCOME		

SAVINGS

(Describe)	
TOTAL SAVINGS	

INVESTMENTS/RETIREMENT

TOTAL INVESTMENTS	

FOOD · HOUSEHOLD · TRANSPORTATION · PERSONAL · MEDICAL

	groceries	meals out, school lunches	tobacco alcohol snacks beverages	mainten. house yard pool	appliances furniture furnishings supplies	misc. postage copies bank chg. film	interest taxes	gas	auto mainten. wash license	transit tolls parking	clothing alterations dry clean. laundry shoe care	toiletries cosmetics hair nails massage	doctor dentist medicine vitamins	personal growth therapy
WEEK 1 — 1														
2														
3														
4														
5														
6														
7														
WEEK 2 — 8														
9														
10														
11														
12														
13														
14														
WEEK 3 — 15														
16														
17														
18														
19														
20														
21														
WEEK 4 — 22														
23														
24														
25														
26														
27														
28														
29														
30														
31														
Total														

MONTHLY EXPENSE RECORD

FIXED EXPENSES

Monthly	Amount	Monthly	Amount
Mortgage/Rent		Insurance:	
Assn. Fee		House/Apt	
Gas/Fuel		Auto	
Electricity		Life	
Water/Refuse		Health	
Garbage/Sewer		Dental	
Telephone		Disability	
Cellular Phone			
Cable/Satellite			
Internet			
Child Support			
Spousal Support			
TOTAL		**TOTAL**	

INSTALLMENT EXPENSES

Loans/Credit Cards	Amount
TOTAL	

TOTAL EXPENSES

Total Fixed Expenses	
Total Installment Expenses	
Total Monthly Expenses from Below	
GRAND TOTAL	

RECREATION · EDUCATION · CHILDREN · GENERAL

	vacation trips	entertain. video movie tapes CDs	lottery sports hobbies lessons clubs	computer upgrades software supplies service	seminar workshop tuition supplies	books magazines software	child care sitter	tutor allowance toys school expense	pet vet supplies	gifts cards flowers	charitable contribut. church	work expense dues	prof. services legal CPA investment	other (expla-nation)
1														
2														
3														
4														
5														
6														
7														
8														
9														
10														
11														
12														
13														
14														
15														
16														
17														
18														
19														
20														
21														
22														
23														
24														
25														
26														
27														
28														
29														
30														
31														
Total														

MONTHLY EXPENSE RECORD

Balance Forward from Last Month:
Cash _____ Checking _____ Savings _____

NET INCOME

			TOTAL
SALARY/COMMISSIONS			
TOTAL INCOME			
OTHER			
TOTAL INCOME			

SAVINGS

(Describe)	
TOTAL SAVINGS	

INVESTMENTS/RETIREMENT

TOTAL INVESTMENTS	

FOOD — HOUSEHOLD — TRANSPORTATION — PERSONAL — MEDICAL

	groceries	meals out, school lunches	tobacco alcohol snacks beverages	mainten. house yard pool	appliances furniture furnishings supplies	misc. postage copies bank chg. film	interest taxes	gas	auto mainten. wash license	transit tolls parking	clothing alterations dry clean. laundry shoe care	toiletries cosmetics hair nails massage	doctor dentist medicine vitamins	personal growth therapy
WEEK 1 1														
2														
3														
4														
5														
6														
7														
WEEK 2 8														
9														
10														
11														
12														
13														
14														
WEEK 3 15														
16														
17														
18														
19														
20														
21														
WEEK 4 22														
23														
24														
25														
26														
27														
28														
29														
30														
31														
Total														

MONTHLY EXPENSE RECORD

FIXED EXPENSES

Monthly	Amount	Monthly	Amount
Mortgage/Rent		Insurance:	
Assn. Fee		House/Apt	
Gas/Fuel		Auto	
Electricity		Life	
Water/Refuse		Health	
Garbage/Sewer		Dental	
Telephone		Disability	
Cellular Phone			
Cable/Satellite			
Internet			
Child Support			
Spousal Support			
TOTAL		**TOTAL**	

INSTALLMENT EXPENSES

Loans/Credit Cards	Amount
TOTAL	

TOTAL EXPENSES

Total Fixed Expenses	
Total Installment Expenses	
Total Monthly Expenses from Below	
GRAND TOTAL	

RECREATION — EDUCATION — CHILDREN — GENERAL

	vacation trips	entertain. video movie tapes CDs	lottery sports hobbies lessons clubs	computer upgrades software supplies service	seminar workshop tuition supplies	books magazines software	child care sitter	tutor allowance toys school expense	pet vet supplies	gifts cards flowers	charitable contribut. church	work expense dues	prof. services legal CPA investment	other (expla-nation)
1														
2														
3														
4														
5														
6														
7														
8														
9														
10														
11														
12														
13														
14														
15														
16														
17														
18														
19														
20														
21														
22														
23														
24														
25														
26														
27														
28														
29														
30														
31														
Total														

MONTHLY EXPENSE RECORD

Balance Forward from Last Month:
Cash _____ Checking _____ Savings _____

NET INCOME

			TOTAL
SALARY/COMMISSIONS			
		TOTAL INCOME	
OTHER			
		TOTAL INCOME	

SAVINGS

(Describe)	
TOTAL SAVINGS	

INVESTMENTS/RETIREMENT

TOTAL INVESTMENTS	

FOOD — HOUSEHOLD — TRANSPORTATION — PERSONAL — MEDICAL

	groceries	meals out, school lunches	tobacco alcohol snacks beverages	mainten. house yard pool	appliances furniture furnishings supplies	misc. postage copies bank chg. film	interest taxes	gas	auto mainten. wash license	transit tolls parking	clothing alterations dry clean. laundry shoe care	toiletries cosmetics hair nails massage	doctor dentist medicine vitamins	personal growth therapy
W 1														
E 2														
E 3														
K 4														
5														
1 6														
7														
W 8														
E 9														
E 10														
K 11														
12														
2 13														
14														
W 15														
E 16														
E 17														
K 18														
19														
3 20														
21														
W 22														
E 23														
E 24														
K 25														
26														
4 27														
28														
29														
30														
31														
Total														

MONTHLY EXPENSE RECORD

FIXED EXPENSES

Monthly	Amount	Monthly	Amount
Mortgage/Rent		Insurance:	
Assn. Fee		House/Apt	
Gas/Fuel		Auto	
Electricity		Life	
Water/Refuse		Health	
Garbage/Sewer		Dental	
Telephone		Disability	
Cellular Phone			
Cable/Satellite			
Internet			
Child Support			
Spousal Support			
TOTAL		**TOTAL**	

INSTALLMENT EXPENSES

Loans/Credit Cards	Amount
TOTAL	

TOTAL EXPENSES

Total Fixed Expenses	
Total Installment Expenses	
Total Monthly Expenses from Below	
GRAND TOTAL	

RECREATION   EDUCATION   CHILDREN   GENERAL

	vacation trips	entertain. video movie tapes CDs	lottery sports hobbies lessons clubs	computer upgrades software supplies service	seminar workshop tuition supplies	books magazines software	child care sitter	tutor allowance toys school expense	pet vet supplies	gifts cards flowers	charitable contribut. church	work expense dues	prof. services legal CPA investment	other (expla- nation)
1														
2														
3														
4														
5														
6														
7														
8														
9														
10														
11														
12														
13														
14														
15														
16														
17														
18														
19														
20														
21														
22														
23														
24														
25														
26														
27														
28														
29														
30														
31														
Total														

MONTHLY EXPENSE RECORD

Balance Forward from Last Month:
Cash _____ Checking _____ Savings _____

NET INCOME

			TOTAL
SALARY/COMMISSIONS			
TOTAL INCOME			
OTHER			
TOTAL INCOME			

SAVINGS

(Describe)	
TOTAL SAVINGS	

INVESTMENTS/RETIREMENT

TOTAL INVESTMENTS	

	FOOD		HOUSEHOLD						TRANSPORTATION			PERSONAL		MEDICAL	
	groceries	meals out, school lunches	tobacco alcohol snacks beverages	mainten. house yard pool	appliances furniture furnishings supplies	misc. postage copies bank chg. film	interest taxes	gas	auto mainten. wash license	transit tolls parking	clothing alterations dry clean. laundry shoe care	toiletries cosmetics hair nails massage	doctor dentist medicine vitamins	personal growth therapy
W 1															
E 2															
E 3															
K 4															
5															
1 6															
7															
W 8															
E 9															
E 10															
K 11															
12															
2 13															
14															
W 15															
E 16															
E 17															
K 18															
19															
3 20															
21															
W 22															
E 23															
E 24															
K 25															
26															
4 27															
28															
29															
30															
31															
Total															

MONTHLY EXPENSE RECORD

FIXED EXPENSES

Monthly	Amount	Monthly	Amount
Mortgage/Rent		Insurance:	
Assn. Fee		House/Apt	
Gas/Fuel		Auto	
Electricity		Life	
Water/Refuse		Health	
Garbage/Sewer		Dental	
Telephone		Disability	
Cellular Phone			
Cable/Satellite			
Internet			
Child Support			
Spousal Support			
TOTAL		**TOTAL**	

INSTALLMENT EXPENSES

Loans/Credit Cards	Amount
TOTAL	

TOTAL EXPENSES

Total Fixed Expenses	
Total Installment Expenses	
Total Monthly Expenses from Below	
GRAND TOTAL	

RECREATION   EDUCATION   CHILDREN   GENERAL

	vacation trips	entertain. video movie tapes CDs	lottery sports hobbies lessons clubs	computer upgrades software supplies service	seminar workshop tuition supplies	books magazines software	child care sitter	tutor allowance toys school expense	pet vet supplies	gifts cards flowers	charitable contribut. church	work expense dues	prof. services legal CPA investment	other (explanation)
1														
2														
3														
4														
5														
6														
7														
8														
9														
10														
11														
12														
13														
14														
15														
16														
17														
18														
19														
20														
21														
22														
23														
24														
25														
26														
27														
28														
29														
30														
31														
Total														

MONTHLY EXPENSE RECORD

Balance Forward from Last Month:
Cash _____ Checking _____ Savings _____

NET INCOME

			TOTAL
SALARY/COMMISSIONS			
		TOTAL INCOME	
OTHER			
		TOTAL INCOME	

SAVINGS

(Describe)	
TOTAL SAVINGS	

INVESTMENTS/RETIREMENT

TOTAL INVESTMENTS	

FOOD   HOUSEHOLD   TRANSPORTATION   PERSONAL   MEDICAL

	groceries	meals out, school lunches	tobacco alcohol snacks beverages	mainten. house yard pool	appliances furniture furnishings supplies	misc. postage copies bank chg. film	interest taxes	gas	auto mainten. wash license	transit tolls parking	clothing alterations dry clean. laundry shoe care	toiletries cosmetics hair nails massage	doctor dentist medicine vitamins	personal growth therapy
WEEK 1 — 1														
2														
3														
4														
5														
6														
7														
WEEK 2 — 8														
9														
10														
11														
12														
13														
14														
WEEK 3 — 15														
16														
17														
18														
19														
20														
21														
WEEK 4 — 22														
23														
24														
25														
26														
27														
28														
29														
30														
31														
Total														

MONTHLY EXPENSE RECORD

FIXED EXPENSES

Monthly	Amount	Monthly	Amount
Mortgage/Rent		Insurance:	
Assn. Fee		House/Apt	
Gas/Fuel		Auto	
Electricity		Life	
Water/Refuse		Health	
Garbage/Sewer		Dental	
Telephone		Disability	
Cellular Phone			
Cable/Satellite			
Internet			
Child Support			
Spousal Support			
TOTAL		**TOTAL**	

INSTALLMENT EXPENSES

Loans/Credit Cards	Amount
TOTAL	

TOTAL EXPENSES

Total Fixed Expenses	
Total Installment Expenses	
Total Monthly Expenses from Below	
GRAND TOTAL	

RECREATION   EDUCATION   CHILDREN   GENERAL

	entertain. video movie tapes CDs	lottery sports hobbies lessons clubs	computer upgrades software supplies service	seminar workshop tuition supplies	books magazines software	child care sitter	tutor allowance toys school expense	pet vet supplies	gifts cards flowers	charitable contribut. church	work expense dues	prof. services legal CPA investment	other (expla-nation)
	vacation trips												
1													
2													
3													
4													
5													
6													
7													
8													
9													
10													
11													
12													
13													
14													
15													
16													
17													
18													
19													
20													
21													
22													
23													
24													
25													
26													
27													
28													
29													
30													
31													
Total													

Summary-for-the-Year Record/ End-of-the-Year Tax Information

The totals you have at the end of each month on the **Monthly Expense Record** can be transferred to this section so you will have a total picture and a way to compare monthly expenses for each category. This **Summary-for-the-Year Record** is excellent for measuring your financial progress and setting your future goals. The End-of-the-Year Tax Information worksheet offers a place to record your pay stub withdrawal information.

SUMMARY-FOR-THE-YEAR RECORD

		JAN.	FEB.	MAR.	APR.	MAY	JUNE	JULY	AUG.	SEPT.	OCT.	NOV.	DEC.	Total	Mo. Avg.
Net Income	Salary/Commission														
	Other														
Food	Groceries														
	School Lunches, Meals Out														
	Snacks, Beverages, Alcohol, Tobacco														
Household	Supplies, Maintenance, House, Yard, Pool														
	Appliances, Furniture, Furnishings, Supplies														
	Postage, Copies Bank Charges, Film, Miscellaneous														
	Interest, Taxes														
Transportation	Gas														
	Automobile Maintenance, Wash, License														
	Transit, Tolls, Parking														
Personal	Clothing, Alterations, Dry cleaning, Laundry, Shoe Care														
	Cosmetics, Hair, Nails, Massage, Toiletries														
Medical	Doctor, Dentist, Medicine, Vitamins														
	Personal Growth Therapy														
Recreation	Vacation, Trips														
	Entertain., Video, Movies, Tapes, CDS														
	Sports, Hobbies, Lessons, Clubs, Lottery														
	Computer, Upgrades, Sofware, Supplies, Service														

SUMMARY FOR MONTHLY SAVINGS/ INVESTMENTS/RETIREMENTS

	JAN.	FEB.	MAR.	APR.	MAY	JUNE	JULY	AUG.	SEPT.	OCT.	NOV.	DEC.	Total
Savings													
Investments													
Retirement													
Total													

		JAN.	FEB.	MAR.	APR.	MAY	JUNE	JULY	AUG.	SEPT.	OCT.	NOV.	DEC.	Total	Mo. Avg.
Education	Tuition, Supplies, Workshops, Seminars														
Education	Books, Magazines Software														
Children	Child Care, Sitter														
Children	Allowance, Toys, School Expense, Tutor														
General	Pet, Vet, Supplies														
General	Gifts, Cards, Flowers														
General	Charitable Contribut., Church														
General	Work Expense, Dues														
General	Prof. Serv., Legal, CPA, Investment														
General	Other														
Home	Mortgage, Rent, Assn. Fees														
Utilities	Gas, Electric														
Utilities	Water, Garbage														
Utilities	Phone, Cable, ISP														
Support	Child, Spousal														
Insurance	Home, Auto, Life, Health, Disability														
Installment	Loans, Credit Cards														
Total	Monthly Expenses														

END-OF-THE-YEAR TAX INFORMATION

	JAN.	FEB.	MAR.	APR.	MAY	JUNE	JULY	AUG.	SEPT.	OCT.	NOV.	DEC.	Total
Federal													
State													
FICA													
Other Deductions													
Total													

Part Three

Medical Expense Record

Tax-Deductible Expense Record

Miscellaneous Expense Record

Investment/Savings Record

Child Support Records

Subscription Record

Online and Mail Order Purchase Record

This collection of worksheets for keeping records and recording expenses will help you keep your financial records organized. Look through each of these forms to see which worksheets apply to you and will be helpful for your particular household's financial situation.

Medical Expense Record

If you need to keep additional records on medical expenses, use these worksheets. The first page, Doctor, Dentist, and Hospital Visits, can be used for recording all visits including nontraditional health care. Include the costs here whether they are full pay, co-pay, or are going to be reimbursed by insurance. If you have a lot of prescriptions, lab tests, and other related medical expenses (like glasses, crutches, rental medical equipment, etc.), then use the second page, Medical Expenses, Prescriptions, and Other to keep those expense records separate.

Again, these worksheets are a guideline so adjust them to work for your medical recordkeeping needs.

A space is provided for mileage, which at this writing is tax-deductible. The columns for "Date Submitted" and "Insurance Reimbursements" are provided for those households paying the medical bills first before submitting claims or paying the differences not covered by insurance and wanting to keep this information separate.

During tax time this information will save you hours of preparation time.

MEDICAL EXPENSE RECORD

DOCTOR, DENTIST, AND HOSPITAL VISITS

Date	Mileage	To Whom Paid	Amount	Date Submitted	Insurance Reimbursements Amount/Date Paid
			Total		
			Total Amount Paid		
			Total Reimbursed		
			Total Medical Cost		

MEDICAL EXPENSE RECORD

MEDICAL EXPENSES, PRESCRIPTIONS, AND OTHER

Date	Mileage	To Whom Paid	Amount	Date Submitted	Insurance Reimbursements Amount/Date Paid
Total					
Total Amount Paid					
Total Reimbursed					
Total Medical Cost					

Tax-Deductible Expense Record

After you record your expenses on the **Monthly Expense Record** worksheets, take a moment to jot down deductible expenses on the Tax-Deductible Expense Record so you have all your deductible expenses recorded in one place. When you prepare next year's tax return, itemizing deductions will be a very quick and efficient process.

Each year, tax deductions may vary. This worksheet is designed to be a convenient record of all deductions applying to your circumstances and the current tax laws. Include categories such as education, professional or union dues, child care, alimony, casualty losses, etc. If you have regular or multiple deductions in one category, the Multiple Tax-Deductible Expense Record may be more convenient for recording those amounts.

Consult your tax professional regarding any changes in tax law for these or any other tax-related records.

The IRS audited my records and said they were so good it was no problem and they accepted all of it. My insurance company also accepted my records without having receipts. I'm 68 years old and have used this book for ten years and I'm buying ten more for the next ten years.

TAX-DEDUCTIBLE EXPENSE RECORD

Date	Description (Donation/Payment To)	Check Number	Amount/Value: Taxes/ Interest	Charitable Contribution		
	Total					

MULTIPLE TAX-DEDUCTIBLE EXPENSES RECORD

CATEGORY:		
Date	Description	Amount
	Total	

CATEGORY:		
Date	Description	Amount
	Total	

Miscellaneous Expense Record

A variety of additional generic worksheets are provided for other records such as major household purchases, home improvement projects, car expenses, college costs, etc. Use any of these or the other variety of worksheets in this workbook to best fit your particular needs.

RECORD OF _____ MISCELLANEOUS EXPENSE RECORD YEAR 20___

	JAN.	FEB.	MAR.	APR.	MAY	JUNE	JULY	AUG.	SEPT.	OCT.	NOV.	DEC.	**TOTAL**
Total													

MISCELLANEOUS EXPENSE RECORD

Date	To Whom Paid/Service	Amount
	Total	

Date	To Whom Paid/Service	Amount
	Total	

Investment/ Savings Record

YOUR INVESTMENT PICTURE

If you followed the suggestions and guidelines in this workbook, you probably already have or soon will have some basic savings and investments.

Whether you have money in company savings plans, inherited some stocks and bonds, invested in mutual funds, changed your savings from passbooks to certificates of deposit (CDs) or money markets, or opened an individual retirement account (IRA), it is important to keep all your records in one place and know what you have. These records are extremely useful for preparing income tax, completing financial statements, and helping your heirs in the event of an unexpected death.

As with personal finances, if you don't pay attention to your investments or keep careful records of them, you may easily forget what you have or where you have them. Soon it may be hard to remember just exactly where you put those IRAs that you purchased sometime in 1988 or 1991. What rates are they getting? What are the maturity dates?

Or maybe through your parents or a divorce, you acquired some stocks that are just "sitting" in an account and you really don't know what you have. With today's fast-paced lifestyle, it is easy to leave the responsibility of knowing what you own to someone else—a banker, a broker, or an accountant—but by doing so, you sacrifice an understanding and awareness of your total financial picture.

The **Investment/Savings Record** provides a place for recording key information about your various investments. The space on the right allows for a periodic follow-up of your current yield. The headings are

used as a guideline. If necessary, change them to make them appropriate for your investments.

If you anticipate frequent changes, you should record general information at the beginning of the year here and use the other worksheets in this section of the workbook to record your investment and savings activity. You can modify the **Savings Activity Record, Retirement Savings Record,** or **Miscellaneous Expense Record** to fit your needs. The important point is to be sure that you have recorded all the information for each of your investments and have it all in one convenient place.

RESERVE FUNDS

Use this section of the Investment/Savings Record to record information about your liquid-asset accounts (money you have available for immediate use without withdrawal penalties). These include investments in money market accounts or savings in your bank and/or credit union.

If you have ongoing monthly savings activity, you can use the **Savings Activity Record** to record your month-to-month transactions. On that page, you can list your savings for upcoming taxes or insurance (reserve account), unexpected car or home repairs (emergency account), or vacation and Christmas/holiday savings (goal account).

RETIREMENT

Record the information for your retirement savings programs here. Your monthly savings activity can be recorded on the **Retirement Savings Record** in this section. These programs range from savings funded and/or established by your employer, to personal IRAs, Keoghs, tax-sheltered annuities (TSAs), company pensions, and other tax-sheltered investments.

A wide variety of employee-retirement programs are offered through schools, hospitals, government, and private firms. It is easy to forget or ignore these funds for they often are only shown as paycheck deductions. Pay attention to and gather up the necessary information as outlined in this section so you are familiar with your current and past retirement programs.

SHORT- AND LONG-TERM HOLDINGS

Record your investments held for short or extended periods on the **Investment/Savings Record.** Some of these investments, such as certificates of deposit (CDs), T-bills, bonds, etc., will have fixed rates or time periods and this information should be noted on the worksheet. Other securities (stocks, mutual funds, options) may change yields, time frames, and prices daily. Because there is limited space for all the variable information, use this worksheet for beginning- and end-of-the-year summaries.

If you frequently buy, sell, and actively get involved with your investments, you already may have an investment portfolio with all the necessary information. On the other hand, if you do not do much with your investments, especially securities, *the information on*

this worksheet will be extremely helpful for tax, loan, or net worth purposes.

OTHER INVESTMENTS

Your investments, such as real estate (other than personal residence), collectibles, trusts, limited or general partnerships, etc., also would be recorded here. If the majority of those other investments are quite extensive, however, you probably have them recorded through another system. If so, indicate where you have those records. The same is true for any of your other investments listed on this worksheet.

MAINTAINING CONTROL OF YOUR FINANCES

As you gather your investment information, you may find you need to develop your own follow-up system for those long-range investments with maturity dates. Start a file and keep a copy of these worksheets for each year. Highlight the maturity dates so you have a quick reference.

While reviewing your investments, take time to monitor the returns and determine how well your investments are performing.

These worksheets, along with the others you have used in this workbook, will help you to record all your financial information in one place, thus staying organized and aware of your finances.

INVESTMENT/SAVINGS RECORD

RESERVE FUNDS (Checking, Savings, Money Market, etc.)

Name of Institution	Type	Account Number	Date Opened	Amount Invested	Interest Rate	Owned By (husband, wife, joint)

RETIREMENT ACCOUNTS (IRA, TSA, 401(k), 403(b), SEP, Keogh, etc.)

Where Held	Type and Name	Account Number	Purchase Date	Amount Invested	Interest Rate	Maturity Date

SHORT- AND LONG-TERM HOLDINGS (Mutual Funds, Stocks, Bonds, etc.)

Where Held	Type and Name	Certificate/ Account Number	Purchase Date	Amount Invested	Number of Shares	Unit Price	Dividend/ Interest Rate

OTHER (Real Estate, Collectibles, etc.)

Location/Name	Date Purchased	Cost	Monthly/Yearly Income	Location of Records

INVESTMENT/SAVINGS RECORD

RESERVE FUNDS

Contact Name/Telephone	Location of Records	Follow-Up Information (date, balance, current yield)

RETIREMENT ACCOUNTS

Owned By (husband, wife, joint)	Contact Name/Telephone	Location of Records	Date Sold	Net Proceeds	Gain/ Loss	Additional Notes (rollover information)

SHORT- AND LONG-TERM HOLDINGS

Date/Amount Dividend Paid	Maturity Date	Owned By (husband, wife, joint)	Contact Name/Telephone	Location of Records	Date Sold	Number of Shares Sold	Net Proceeds	Gain/ Loss

OTHER

Additional Notes (date sold, total proceeds, etc.)

SAVINGS ACTIVITY RECORD

EMERGENCY

Institution: _____   Account Number: _____

	JAN.	FEB.	MAR.	APR.	MAY	JUNE	JULY	AUG.	SEPT.	OCT.	NOV.	DEC.
Deposits												
Withdrawals												
Interest Earned												
Balance												

RESERVE

Institution: _____   Account Number: _____

	JAN.	FEB.	MAR.	APR.	MAY	JUNE	JULY	AUG.	SEPT.	OCT.	NOV.	DEC.
Deposits												
Withdrawals												
Interest Earned												
Balance												

GOALS/CHRISTMAS AND HOLIDAY

Institution: _____   Account Number: _____

	JAN.	FEB.	MAR.	APR.	MAY	JUNE	JULY	AUG.	SEPT.	OCT.	NOV.	DEC.
Deposits												
Withdrawals												
Interest Earned												
Balance												

OTHER

Institution: _____   Account Number: _____

	JAN.	FEB.	MAR.	APR.	MAY	JUNE	JULY	AUG.	SEPT.	OCT.	NOV.	DEC.
Deposits												
Withdrawals												
Interest Earned												
Balance												

RETIREMENT SAVINGS RECORD

NAME

Date	Program (IRA, 401(k), etc.): ___ ___ ___			Program (IRA, 401(k) etc.): Date ___ ___ ___		
Total				**Total**		

NAME

Date	Program (IRA, 401(k), etc.): ___ ___ ___			Program (IRA, 401(k) etc.): Date ___ ___ ___		
Total				**Total**		

Child Support Records

Earlier this year I needed a personal loan. I couldn't have qualified if I had no proof of child support. The record in this workbook was sufficient information for the bank's approval.

KEEPING RECORDS

After a divorce, it is so easy for depression, anger, fear, and loneliness to interfere with practical thoughts and actions.

During this time, credit problems often crop up. This is not because you are incapable of managing your money, but often because you suddenly are overwhelmed with handling all the aspects of family life and household maintenance. Due dates, bills, and paperwork may just seem to get away from you.

Keeping proper records of child support payments, children's expenses, and pertinent custody information is extremely important. However, because of the demands of trying to meet the physical and emotional needs of your children and yourself, these records often are neglected or are never established.

The following worksheets were designed to help remove some of the burden of keeping important records. The worksheets provide guidelines to help you remember what records you should keep and provide you with a tool for having all your necessary information and records in one place. By organizing and controlling this aspect of your life, you will be better equipped to move on to other pressing issues that you face every day.

If you are the noncustodial parent making the child support payments, recording the information called

for can be just as important for you. If you must prove what amount and when a support payment actually was made, received, and cashed, or must prove other significant information for tax or legal purposes, you will have the necessary records.

Utilize and modify the worksheets in this book so that you can record information that is unique to your needs. For example, you may want to use the Medical and Dental Expense section of this workbook for keeping detailed records of who paid a medical expense, the insurance deductible, or the difference not paid by insurance.

When using these worksheets, be aware that the state and federal laws and regulations vary. *The worksheets and text are not a substitute for legal advice from your local attorney. Consult with your attorney for any questions in this section.*

CHILD SUPPORT PAYMENT RECORD

This record is critical when you need help from your local enforcement agency because of late, short, or missing payments. The "Amount Due" column is ① for the monthly child support payment as ordered. Enter the amount received under the month it was *due*. If no payment was received that month, note that under "Amount Received." Because these payments ② may vary from once a week, or once a month, to sporadically for the year, you will have to modify this column to fit your needs.

Record the other related child support obligations ③ as ordered by the divorce decree, such as medical insurance premium, unreimbursed medical expense, tuition, dues, etc. Also keep records of conversations concerning finances with your case workers, ex-spouse, and others. Keep a copy of your decree, stating the terms, payment, custody, visitation, conditions of support, and your record of conversations in a convenient file.

④ Note under "Additional Information" if an item was substituted in lieu of a child support payment. Be sure to check with your attorney if this is an *acceptable form of child support*. If you do not wish to accept an item in lieu of a payment, ask your attorney if written notice should be given. If so, be sure to keep a copy.

⑤ When recording the institution, number, and date of the check or money order, use the symbols shown to indicate how the payment was made. If possible, keep a copy of all checks, money orders, and envelopes, especially if there is a regular problem with support being on time. These copies will be helpful if a court or social agency ever needs to review your records in the event that there is an excessive lag between the date of the check and the date it was sent, or payment was stopped on a check or money order you received. Be sure to note if you are unable to make a copy of the checks, money orders, or envelopes.

You will find that this worksheet will contain some of your most important records. Stay with it.

THE COST OF RAISING CHILDREN

If you need or want to analyze the cost of raising your children, to show the use of support provided, or to demonstrate the need for increased support, use the **Monthly Expense Record** section.

Enter all your children's daily expenses along with all your other expenses on the Monthly Expense Record pages. Modify the headings to fit your individual needs. Use a highlighter, colored pencil, or check mark to show which expenses are the children's. Total the children's expenses in the columns that apply and record the total at the bottom of the page below the family total. If you have a question about allocating expenses shared by you and your children, ask your local attorney.

Another method used by some families for keeping accurate records is a separate checking account and/or a credit card used strictly for children's expenses. Use the method that works best for you.

If you save all your receipts in envelopes labeled for the different categories, you can file these in your filing system.

CHILD SUPPORT ENFORCEMENT AND CHILD VISITATION RECORDS

In 1984, Congress passed the Child Support Enforcement Amendments of 1984 that strengthen the child support enforcement laws throughout the country. The information you record will be invaluable if you ever need the services of a Child Support Enforcement Bureau in your state to help you collect past-due child support.

If you would like more information about Child Support Enforcement, write the Consumer Information Center, Dept. 633 B, Pueblo, CO 81009, and ask for a free copy of "Kids, They're Worth Every Penny: Handbook on Child Support Enforcement," provided by the Office of Child Support Enforcement in Washington, D.C.

A basic **Child Visitation Record** is provided if you need a way to record specific dates of visitation each month.

For a more extensive way to keep track of time sharing, holidays, school activities, and other important events being shared between two households, order "My Two Homes—The Divorce Calendar for Kids" ($20.90), LadyBug Press, P.O. Box 7249, Albuquerque, NM 87102-7249, 800-244-1761. This is a great calendar that was developed by an attorney. With its design and hundreds of colorful stickers, it gives kids whose parents are divorced a visual and fun way to know their schedules. You can start it any time of the year. See their Web site <www.mytwohomes.com> for more great products.

REDUCED ANXIETY

These worksheets cannot take away the pain. They can, however, help reduce some of the anxiety associated with the aftermath of a divorce. As you start taking charge of your situation and gain new knowledge, you will regain self-confidence and self-esteem in the process.

Best of luck to you!

CHILD SUPPORT PAYMENT RECORD

Balance Due (from previous year) $_____

Month	① Amount Due	② Amount Received	Amount Past Due	⑤ Number on: x—$ Order ✓—Check $—Cash	Date on: x—$ Order ✓—Check $—Cash	⑤ Date Payment Received	Institution and Account Number	③ Other Expenses*	④ Additional Information/ Action Taken (check status, gifts, etc.)
JAN.									
FEB.									
MAR.									
APR.									
MAY									
JUNE									
JULY									
AUG.									
SEPT.									
OCT.									
NOV.									
DEC.									
Total									

*Stipulated by decree

CHILD SUPPORT ENFORCEMENT RECORD

Child Support Enforcement Office

Full Name
_____

Occupation
_____

Last Known Address(es)
_____
_____
_____

Address Dates_____

Home Telephone
_____

Social Security Number
_____

Birth Date/Place _____
_____

Height _____ Weight _____

Last Known Employer(s)
_____
_____

Address
_____
_____
_____

Address Dates_____

Work Telephone
_____
_____

Address
_____
_____

Telephone Number
_____

Case Worker's Name/Telephone
_____
_____

Case Number
_____

Court Order Number
_____

Note: Get a Birth Registration Card from your Vital Statistics Office. This will have all your children's information printed on it so you will have the information handy.

CHILD VISITATION RECORD

DATES OF VISITATION

JAN.	FEB.	MAR.	APR.	MAY	JUNE	JULY	AUG.	SEPT.	OCT.	NOV.	DEC.

Subscription Record

If you ever waited three months to receive your subscription or learned that your magazine gift took that long before it was ever received, you will appreciate having all this information at your fingertips.

Having this record is an easy way to organize all your subscription amounts and dates due in one central place. It also will help prevent any double payments. You can then transfer this information to the **Yearly Budget Worksheet** in Part Two where all your nonmonthly expenses are listed on one convenient page.

SUBSCRIPTION RECORD

Publication:						
Subscription Through: Agency Address						
Telephone						
Date Ordered						
Amount Paid						
Check # or Credit Card Used						
Length (1, 2, 3 yrs.)						
Expiration Date						
Arrival Date						
Gift For:						
Other						

Online and Mail Order Purchase Record

SHOPPING BY MAIL OR INTERNET

There are obvious advantages to shopping by mail or online, including convenience, saving time, and discount savings. However, how many times have you ordered something by mail or telephone or now by Internet, trusting that it would arrive and it never did? Chances are you have had your share of mail order frustrations and undelivered orders and maybe even forgotten orders. If so, now you probably can recognize the value of keeping records for follow-up action.

HOW TO KEEP RECORDS

If orders do not arrive as scheduled and follow-up action is necessary, this Online and Mail Order Purchase Record will be a valuable time and money saver for you.

Use this form for all items ordered even if they are free. Keeping track of rebates also will work on this form. Log the necessary information related to any purchases made by mail, telephone, or online. When you happen to remember an item you ordered some time ago and realize it still has not arrived, you can check these records, see when you ordered the item, then follow up by the appropriate method.

In some cases, it may be easier to cut out the ad with all the information given and tape it to this page or in the back of this workbook. Then fill in only the "Total Sent" and "How Paid" sections. If you order a list of items from one catalog, make a copy of the order form and save it. On this page, make a note of the order, the catalog date, and how and when you paid for it. The same is true for online orders. Print out a copy of the order, including the confirmation number, and save that copy with your records or in the back of this workbook.

When placing a telephone order or following up on an order, be especially careful to record all the information on this worksheet, including the name of the person you spoke to or who took your order.

SAFETY ONLINE

Shop with the companies you know. If you want to learn more about an unfamiliar company before ordering, ask them to send you information or a catalog. Be sure to find out the company's policies on refunds and returns before placing any order.

Find out if your browser is secure before purchasing anything online. Note if there is a lock icon on the bottom corner of the screen. Some browsers use a closed lock icon to indicate a secure session. A secured session is extremely important when you provide personal information such as credit card number, name, address, and phone number over the Internet.

Remember, if you pay with a credit card and have problems with your order, you have the advantage of having the right to dispute your charges. Your creditor will investigate the circumstances while you temporarily withhold payment. The complaint and situation will need to be explained and submitted in writing. Having the records on this page will make that process easier for you.

Be careful with your password. Never give it to anyone. Use a password you can readily remember, but is not as obvious as your birthday, telephone number, license, or Social Security number.

Enjoy these conveniences that now exist, but do so with appropriate caution.

FEDERAL TRADE COMMISSSION (FTC) MAIL ORDER RULE

The Mail Order Rule of the Federal Trade Commission (FTC) requires companies to ship an order within the time period mentioned in their advertisements. If no time period is given, the company is required to ship an order within 30 days of receipt of your payment. The company must notify you if it cannot make the shipment within 30 days and send you an option notice of either consenting to a delay or canceling the order for a refund.

For a free brochure on the Mail Order Rule, write the Federal Trade Commission, Pennsylvania Avenue N.W. at 6th Street, Washington, D.C. 20580.

ONLINE AND MAIL ORDER PURCHASE RECORD

Date Ordered					
Item(s) Ordered 　　Title 　　Description 　　Number 　　Quantity 　　Color					
Source (Internet, magazine, TV, catalog)					
Company Name 　　Telephone Number 　　Address					
Price					
Total Sent					
How Paid (credit card, check number, money order, C.O.D.)					
Date Received					
Follow-Up Notes (date called/wrote, contact person, action taken)					

ONLINE AND MAIL ORDER PURCHASE RECORD

Date Ordered					

Item(s) Ordered
   Title
   Description
   Number
   Quantity
   Color					

Source (Internet, magazine, TV, catalog)					

Company Name
   Telephone Number
   Address					

Price					
Total Sent					
How Paid (credit card, check number, money order, C.O.D.)					
Date Received					
Follow-Up Notes (date called/wrote, contact person, action taken)					

Recommended Reading

The following books and other resources are included because of their total focus or special sections on *budgeting, credit, debt, spending, money attitudes,* and/or *recovery issues.* If you want more financial planning information, there are numerous excellent books with a full range and comprehensive coverage of all facets of personal finance available at your local book stores, library, or through the Web.

If managing money is new for you, these books offer a variety of ideas, approaches, and information to help you get started. The following books can provide complementary information as you do the practical hands-on part with *The Budget Kit: Common Cent$ Money Management Workbook.*

Beating the Paycheck-to-Paycheck Blues, John Ventura (Dearborn Trade, 1996).

Bill Griffeth's 10 Steps to Financial Prosperity (Warner Books, 1996).

Born to Spend: How to Overcome Compulsive Spending, Gloria Arenson (TAB Books, 1992).

The Cheapskate Monthly Money Makeover, Mary Hunt (St. Martin's Paperbacks, 1995).

The Complete Idiot's Guide to Managing Your Money, Robert K. Heady and Christy Heady (MacMillian Distribution, 1999).

Creating Money: Keys to Abundance, Sanaya Roman and Duane Packer (H. J. Kramer Inc., 1988).

Credit, Cash, and Co-Dependency: The Money Connection, Yvonne Kaye, PhD (Islewest Publishing, 1998).

Cut Your Spending the Lazy Way, Leslie Haggin (alpha books, 1999).

Debt-Proof Living: The Complete Guide to Living Financially Free, Mary Hunt (Broadman and Holman Publishers, 1999).

Downsize Your Debt: How to Take Control of Your Personal Finances, Andrew Feinberg (Penguin Books, 1993).

Every Woman's Guide to Financial Security, Ann Z. Peterson and Stephen M. Rosenberg, CFP (Career Press, 1997).

Financial Fitness for Life Trade: Advice from America's Top Financial Planning Program, Jerry Mason (Dearborn Trade, 1999).

Financial Peace Planner: A Step-by-Step Guide to Restoring Your Family's Financial Health, Dave Ramsey (Penguin Books, 1998).

For Richer, Not Poorer: The Money Book for Couples, Ruth L. Hayden (Health Communications Inc., 1999).

Get Rich Slow, Tama McAleese (Career Press, 1995).

Getting Rich in America: 8 Simple Rules for Building a Fortune and a Satisfying Life, Dwight R. Lee and Richard B. McKenzie (HarperBusiness Book, 1999).

Got money? Enjoy It! Manage It! Even Save Some of It!, Jeff Wuorio (Amacom, 1999).

The Guide to Saving Money, David L. Scott (The Globe Pequot Press, 1996).

How to Get Out of Debt, Stay Out of Debt & Live Prosperously, Jerrold Mundis (Bantam Books, 1990). Based on the proven principles and techniques of Debtors Anonymous.

How to Get What You Want in Life with the Money You Already Have, Carol Keeffe (Little Brown and Company, 1995).

How to Have More than Enough: A Step-by-Step Guide to Creating Abundance, Ten Proven Keys to Increasing Your Wealth and Family Harmony, Dave Ramsey (Penguin Books, 2000).

How to Survive Without a Salary: Learning How to Live the Conserver Lifestyle, Charles Long (Warwick Publishers, 1996).

How to Turn Your Money Life Around: The Money Books for Women, Ruth Hayden (Health Communications Inc., 1992).

Invest in Yourself: Six Secrets to a Rich Life, Marc Eisenson, Gerri Detweiler, and Nancy Castleman (John Wiley and Sons, 1998).

It's Never Too Late to . . . Wake Up and Smell the Money: Fresh Starts at Any Age—and Any Season of your Life, Ginger Applegarth with Leslie Whitaker (Penguin USA, 2000).

It's Your Money: Achieving Financial Well-Being, Karen McCall (Chronicle Books, 2000).

I've Been Rich. I've Been Poor. Rich Is Better. How Every Woman Can Find Economic Security and Personal Freedom, Judy Resnick with Gene Stone (St. Martin's edition, 1999).

Life after Debt: Free Yourself from the Burden of Money Worries Once and for All, Bob Hammond (Career Press, 2000).

Making Peace with Money, Jerrold Mundis (Andrews McMeel Publishing, 1999).

Making the Most of Your Money, Jane Bryant Quinn (Simon & Schuster, 1997).

Mary Hunt's the Complete Cheapskate: How to Get Out of Debt, Stay Out, and Break Free from Money Worries Forever, Mary Hunt (Broadman & Holman Publishers, 1998).

The Mindful Money Guide: Creating Harmony between Your Values and Your Finances, Marshall Glickman (Ballantine Wellspring Publishing Group, 1999).

Money Advice for Your Successful Remarriage: Handling Delicate Financial Issues with Love and Understanding, Patricia Schiff Estess (Betterway Books, 1996).

The Money Diet: Reaping the Rewards of Financial Fitness, Ginger Applegarth (Penguin Books, 1996).

Money Doesn't Grow on Trees: A Parent's Guide to Raising Financially Responsible Children, Neale S. Godfrey and Carolina Edwards (Simon and Schuster, 1994).

Money: How to Get It, Keep It, and Make It Grow, Tama McAleese (Chelsea House Publishers, 1997).

Money Love: How to Get the Money You Deserve for Whatever You Want, Jerry Gilles (Warner Books, 1994).

Money 101: Your Step-by-Step Guide to Enjoying a Secure Future, Debra Wishik Englander (Prima Publishing, 1997).

The 9 Steps to Financial Freedom: Practical and Spiritual Steps So You Can Stop Worrying, Suze Orman (Crown Publishers, Inc., 1997).

Ninety Days to Financial Fitness, Joan German-Grapes (IDG Books Worldwide 1993).

100 Questions You Should Ask about Your Personal Finances and the Answers You Need to Help You Save, Invest, and Grow Your Money, Ilyce R. Glink (Times Business Random House, 1999).

1001 Ways to Cut Your Expenses, Jonathan D. Pond (Dell Books, 1992).

Overcoming Overspending: A Winning Plan for Spenders and Their Partners, Olivia Mellan (Walker and Company, 1997).

Penny Pinching: How to Lower Your Everyday Expenses without Lowering Your Standard of Living, Lee and Barbara Simmons (Bantam Books, 1999).

Personal Finance for Busy People, Robert A. Cooke (McGraw-Hill, 1998).

Personal Finance for Dummies, Eric Tyson (IDG Books, 2000).

Prospering Woman: A Complete Guide to Achieving the Full Abundant Life, Ruth Ross, PhD (New World Library, 1995).

Richest Man in Babylon, George S. Clason (New American Library, 1997).

Simple Money Solutions: 10 Ways You Can Stop Feeling Overwhelmed by Money and Start Making It Work for You, Nancy Lloyd (Times Business Random House, 2000).

Slash Your Debt: Save Money and Secure Your Future, Gerri Detweiler, Marc Eisenson, and Nancy Casleman (Financial Literacy Center, 1999).

The Smart Woman's Guide to Spending, Saving, and Managing Money, Diane Pearl and Ellie Williams Clinton (Harper, 1997).

10 Minute Guide to Beating Debt, Susan Abentrod (IDG Books Worldwide, 1996).

10-Minute Guide to Household Budgeting, Tracey Longo (Macmillan Spectrum Alpha Books, 1997).

The Ultimate Credit Handbook: How to Double Your Credit, Cut Your Debt, and Have a Lifetime of Great Credit, Gerri Detweiler (Plume, 1997).

The Way to Save—A 10-Step Blueprint for Lifetime Security, Ginita Wall (Henry Holt, 1994).

You Can't Pay Your Credit Card Bill with a Credit Card and Other Habits of the Financially Confident Woman, Mary Hunt (Broadman & Holman Publishers, 1996).

Your Wealth-Building Years, Adriane G. Berg (Newmarket Press, 1995).

Online Resources

There are plenty of Web sites available and easy to find when searching in the area of personal finance. The following Web sites have a specific focus or section on general basic money management instead of investing and were available at the time of this writing. Topics include budgeting, credit, debt, spending, saving money, money attitudes, and recovery issues.

A few of the Web sites have very convenient and well-designed calculators for developing basic budgets or calculating debt payoff. Others offer special debt management counseling and payment services. Some provide excellent materials and articles. Good Advice Press and National Center for Financial Education are two such sites that offer a comprehensive list of books, newsletters, and articles. Once you are in these Web sites, there are often many valuable links to add to this list.

American Express
<www.americanexpress.com>

American Savings Education Council
<www.asec.org>

Bankrate.com—Independent, objective financial information
<www.bankrate.com>

Dave Ramsey
<www.daveramsey.com>

Debt Management
<www.debt.com/budget.html>

The Dollar Stretcher: Living Better for Less
<www.stretcher.com>

Family Money Magazine Online
<www.familymoney.com>

Family Resource Center
<www.ourfamilyplace.com>

Federal Consumer Information Center
<www.pueblo.gsa.gov>

financenter.com—Smart personal finance at a click
<www.financenter.com>

Genesis The Financial Services Press
<www.financialcounseling.net>

Genus Credit Management
<www.genus.org>

Good Advice Press
<www.goodadvicepress.com>

Household Budget Management
<www.dacomp.com/budget1.html>

Kiplinger Magazine Online
<www.kiplinger.com>

Mary Hunt's Debt Proof Living
<www.debtproofliving.com>

MoneyAdvisor—Financial calculators
<www.moneyadvisor.com/calc>

MoneyCentral Saving and Spending
<www.moneycentral.msn.com>

The Money Maven: The Women's Financial Forum
<www.themoneymaven.com>

Myvesta.org Nonprofit Financial Help
<www.myvesta.org>

National Center for Financial Education (NCFE)
<www.ncfe.org>

National Foundation for Consumer Credit
<www.nfcc.org>

Organize Your Dollars
<www.organizeyourdollars.com>

Quicken
<www.quicken.com>

Right On the Money
<www.rightonthemoney.org>

The Whiz.com—Personal finance for the rest of us
<www.theWhiz.com>

Women.com Network—The Smart Way to Get
Things Done
<www.women.com>

Yahoo! Finance
<www.Finance.yahoo.com>

Index

About the Author

Judy Lawrence, MS Ed., is a financial counselor and popular speaker on basic money management. She has been a featured guest on numerous television and radio shows throughout the country. *The Budget Kit*, formerly known as *Common Cent$*, was developed in 1981 while she was counseling reentry widowed and divorced women college students with limited budgeting experience. It soon became apparent that budgeting and saving issues were a universal concern to all populations. Judy saw the need for a non-intimidating workbook that could immediately be used by people with limited time or limited organizing and budgeting skills.

In 1986, she started a unique financial budget counseling practice in Albuquerque, New Mexico, where she counseled couples, individuals, and small businesses in addition to being a court-appointed expert developing and evaluating personal budgets in divorce cases. Her techniques and workbooks, including *The Money Tracker, The Family Memory Book*, and *Daily Riches Gratitude Journal*, have all focused on providing basic, encouraging, and extremely user-friendly support.

Judy now lives in Cupertino, California, where she continues to have a national consulting practice by phone and e-mail. She has recently joined Bizfinity, a start-up e-commerce company in Silicon Valley. There she is part of a product management and support team helping small businesses run their business Web stores and accounting on the Web.

To arrange for media interviews with Judy Lawrence, call Karla Powell, senior publicist for Dearborn Trade, at 800-621-9621, extension 4322, or contact her by e-mail at <powell@dearborn.com>. You can also visit Judy's Web site at <www.moneytracker.com> or arrange for speaking engagements or telephone consultations by calling 800-283-4380 or by e-mail at <judycents@aol.com>.